The Utterly, Completely, and Totally Useless
HISTORY FACT-O-PEDIA
A Startling Collection of Historical Trivia You'll *Never* Need to Know!

* *

CHARLOTTE LOWE * with Emma Wilson and Rachel Federman

SKYHORSE PUBLISHING

Skyhorse Publishing books may be purchased in bulk at special discounts for sales promotion, corporate gifts, fund-raising, or educational purposes. Special editions can also be created to specifications. For details, contact the Special Sales Department, Skyhorse Publishing, 307 West 36th Street, 11th Floor, New York, NY 10018 or info@skyhorsepublishing.com.

www.skyhorsepublishing.com

10 9 8 7 6 5 4 3 2 1

Library of Congress Cataloging-in-Publication Data
available on file.

Printed in China by South China Printing Co. Ltd.

Acknowledgments

Charlotte Lowe

First off, thank you to Jeannine and Laura for making this book happen and Emma Wilson for her cowriting and her vast contribution. I'd like to extend my gratitude to Jon for all his support (and patience) throughout the process. Most of all, I'd like to thank all the historians, history enthusiasts, authors, and researchers who've recorded and documented the greatest lives and events of history—without their knowledge, this book would cease to exist.

Emma Wilson

Big thanks goes out to all my friends and family for their support and for listening to me witter on about useless history facts for months on end. And to Mrs. Burke, who stole one afternoon a week to enlighten us as to the importance of modern history and made what was supposed to be an ordinary class a little less dull.

Rachel Federman

Thanks to Charlotte and Emma for letting me be a part of this fun project. I learned more than I should probably admit, and found useless history to be anything but a waste of time. Thanks to Jeannine for dreaming up and launching the book, and to Laura for seeing it through.

Picture Credits

Contents

A (Age of Discovery—Australia)   1

B (Babylon—Buddhism)   26

C (Caligula—Czars)   49

D (Declaration of Independence—Dutch History)   82

E (Earhart—Explorers)   89

F (Falkland Islands—French Revolution)   103

G (Gandhi—Gutenberg)   116

H (Hadrian's Wall—Hungarian Revolution)   132

I (Inca Empire—Islam)   141

J (Jainism—Justinian's Wars)   148

K (Kennedy—Korean War)   153

L (Lee—Lithuania)   164

M (Magna Carta—Mussolini)   167

N (Napoleon—Nuremberg Trials)   186

O (Old North Bridge—Ottoman Empire)   192

P   (Parks—Prussia)   195

Q   (Qin Dynasty—Queen Victoria)   221

R   (Roman Empire—Russian Revolutions)   223

S   (Safavid Dynasty—Sung Dynasty)   226

T   (Tet Offensive—Turks and Turkey)   250

U   (Umar ibn al-Khattab—USSR)   268

V   (Venice—Vikings)   276

W   (Wales—World War II)   280

X   (Xiaoping)   292

Y   (Ypres—Yugoslavia)   293

Z   (Zambia—Zoroastrianism)   297

Bibliography   307

Introduction

"All great historical facts and personages occur, as it were, twice ... the first time as tragedy, the second time as farce."
—Karl Marx

When we were approached to write the *Useless History Fact-O-Pedia*—following hot on the heels of the overwhelmingly successful and informative *Useless Fact-O-Pedia*—our first reaction was one of apprehension. Having already scoured the globe for a compendium of the world's most useless facts, surely there was nothing left for us to uncover?

How wrong we were.

Like many people, our feelings about history were at best indifferent; at worst they conjured up feelings of boredom, loathing, and dread. The mere thought of history brings to mind long hours spent in the classroom with teachers trying in vain to cram as many facts as possible into our thick skulls. Or rainy afternoons spent with grandpa telling us about what he did during the war (and reminding us that we never had it so good), when all we really wanted to do was watch *The Simpsons*.

That being said, once we were left to ponder the merits of history, one thing did spring to mind: it was always the little things that made it interesting. Never mind memorizing the dates of all those significant battles, it was much more fascinating to discover that it could have been Napoleon's hemorrhoids that caused him to lose the Battle of Waterloo. Or that it took three blows of the ax to sever the head of Mary, Queen of Scots. Or that the Nazi Party rallies actually took their inspiration from Harvard cheerleaders. And thus, after some speculative digging, we realized that maybe—just maybe—history did have something to teach us after all!

The publishers were in luck. At least one of us had a rather neglected history degree under her belt and a few dusty history books under her bed. So, armed with a laptop and a library card, it was not long before we tapped the rich seam of knowledge that is embedded in the history of civilization. From the American Civil War to Zoastrianism, we uncovered *thousands* of useless facts that would otherwise be little more than a minor footnote in the annals of history. Did you know that Julius Caesar, Henry II, Charles XI, and Napoleon all suffered from ailurophobia—a fear of cats? Or that Abraham Lincoln was the first U.S. president to have a beard? Or that "Almost" is the largest word in the English language with all the letters in alphabetical order?

Over the course of our research we realized that our attitude toward history was changing. No longer did we think of it as the dull and dusty topic that was the preserve of tired academics. Our heads were now filled with golden nuggets of useless historical facts, which we then used to pepper our everyday conversation and feign a profound knowledge on any given subject.

They say that history often repeats itself and mankind never really seems to learn from his mistakes. That may be true. But if you consider that you may not really learn anything from history, at least with the *Useless History Fact-O-pedia,* you can be heartily entertained along the way!

Age of Discovery

❧ To infinity and beyond! The mid-to-late fifteenth century was known as the Age of Discovery, when European sailors set sail to explore the green sea of darkness. The Portuguese were the first to charter ships, followed by the Spanish. By the late fifteenth to sixteenth century, the British, French, and Dutch embarked on journeys of their own to discover the *Mundus Novus*, or the New World.

❧ As you can imagine, their understanding of geography and environment was far less advanced than it is today. For one, it was a common belief that Africa and Malaysia were connected together. Many people also thought the Indian Ocean was landlocked. Lastly, the oceans were thought to be inhabited by dragons and sea monsters, and ships were alleged to vanish into great holes in the sea.

A

❧ Arrrrr, who goes there? Portuguese maps during this era were the best in Europe and foreign spies in Lisbon often attempted to buy or steal them.

❧ Although many others had been in America before him, Amerigo Vespucci claimed he had discovered the New World. He named it "Amerigo," after himself.

❧ Scurvy was the number one killer of sailors in the Age of Discovery. To try to combat it, Captain James Cook demanded that his men eat up to 20 pounds (9 kg) of onions in a single week.

Agricultural Revolution

❧ The revolution was a period of agricultural development that saw massive and rapid productivity and improvement in farm technology.

❧ Farming tools barely evolved between the eighth and eighteenth centuries. In fact, early Roman plows were considered far better than those commonly used in America 18 centuries later.

❧ Jethro Tull the Inventor (not to be mistaken with the band) invented the seed drill, the horse-drawn hoe, and an improved plow.

❧ In 1830, about 250–300 labor-hours were required to produce 100 bushels (5 acres) of wheat. By 1890, the number of labor hours was reduced by 85 percent.

❧ The invention of barbed wire in 1874 offered fencing of rangeland and ended an era of unrestricted, open-range grazing.

A

Aksum

🐦 Aksum, located southeast of Kush on rugged land on the Red Sea and Indian Ocean, is the name of the Kingdom of Ethiopia that flourished in the centuries before and after the time of Christ.

🐦 The Kingdom of Aksum was the first kingdom south of the Sahara to mint its own coins, some of which were imprinted with slogans such as, "May the country be satisfied."

🐦 Ge'ez whiz! Aksum was the only African Kingdom to have developed a written language at that time. The language, known as Ge'ez, is a form of Arabic.

🐦 The obelisk is considered a defining characteristic of the Aksumite civilization. In the 1930s, Benito Mussolini looted one from the holy city and erected it in Rome. In late April 2005, Aksum's obelisk was returned to Ethiopia.

🐦 The people of ancient Aksum ate a large, flat, pancake-like bread called *injera* made from teff, the country's staple grain.

A

Alexander the Great

~ Alexander the Great, king of Macedonia and conqueror of the Persian Empire, is considered one of the greatest military geniuses of all time and he holds the record for owning the largest amount of land by a single person in world history … a whopping 2,123,562 square miles (5.5 million square km).

~ Loaded … The Persian wealth taken by Alexander was so great, it was believed that 20,000 mules and 4,000 camels were needed just to transport all the gold, silver, and jewels.

~ When he was 13, Alexander's father, Philip II, hired the Greek philosopher Aristotle to be Alexander's personal tutor.

~ Richard Stoneman, author of the book *Alexander the Great: A Life in Legend*, wrote that Alexander was, "perhaps the first human being in recorded history to be seized by the romance of the east."

~ It's been claimed that Alexander the Great untied the Gordian Knot when he was in Gordium, Turkey, in 333 B.C.E. King Midas had tied the Gordian Knot and it was said that the person who untied it would rule all of Asia.

~ Alexander died at age 33, but the cause of his death is unknown.

A

Alfred the Great

❧ King Alfred the Great (who ruled from 871–899) was a great king who defended Anglo-Saxon England from Viking raids, formulated a code of laws, fostered a rebirth of religion, and promoted education.

❧ He is the only English king to be known as "the Great."

❧ His intention was, "To live worthily as long as I live, and after my life to leave to them that should come after, my memory in good works."

❧ To improve literacy, Alfred went to great lengths for a handful of books to be translated from Latin to Anglo-Saxon. He once declared, "that all the youth now in England … may be devoted to learning."

❧ According to his biographer, a Welsh monk named Asser, Alfred was a complex man who suffered from numerous mental and emotional ailments, which we would today classify as obsessive compulsive disorders.

A

Al Qaeda

❧ On March 11, 2004, ten bombs were set off virtually simultaneously in trains carrying commuters into Madrid. One hundred and ninety people died in the attacks and approximately 2,000 people were wounded.

❧ Al Qaeda has the most widely dispersed network in the history of modern terrorism with a presence in nearly 65 countries.

❧ At least 2,985 people were killed in the 9/11 attacks on New York.

❧ Between 2004 and 2008, Al Qaeda claimed responsibility for 313 attacks and the subsequent death of 3,010 people yet only 12 percent of those killed (371 deaths) were Westerners.

❧ Disney postponed its release of *Big Trouble*, starring Tim Allen, out of respect for the 9/11 attack. The comedy was about a group of Miami residents who avert the detonation of a nuclear bomb on an airplane.

❧ Under pressure … When Egypt, Yemen, and Algeria accused Osama Bin Laden of fostering antigovernment organizations within their borders, Saudi officials permanently seized his passport in 1994.

❧ After the 9/11 attacks the United Arab Emirates were identified as being the financial center used by Al Qaeda to transfer money to hijackers.

A

American Civil War

⚬ During the American Civil War (1861-65), it was legal (and socially acceptable) for a man to beat his wife on the condition that the instrument used in the act was no thicker than the thumb. The term "rule of thumb" was born out of this law.

⚬ Ever heard of the old adage of seeing the world through rose-colored lenses? Glasses with colored lenses were used to treat disorders and illness during the mid-1800s. Yellow-tinted glasses were used for syphilis treatment, while blue ones were for insanity. Pink versions were used to treat depression because one would supposedly be happier after looking through them.

⚬ Only one civilian died in the Battle of Gettysburg (1863): 20-year-old Mary Virginia "Jennie" Wade. She was shot through the heart while baking bread. Dough!

A

⚬ More than three million men fought in the war and two percent of the population (60,000) died in it. Disease was the chief killer, taking two men for every one who died of battle wounds.

⚬ Andersonville Prison in southwest Georgia was the fifth-largest military prison in the Confederacy and held 33,000 prisoners by 1864.

American Revolutionary War

A

The Americans of 1776 had the highest standard of living and the lowest taxes in the Western World with some plantation owners and merchants making the equivalent of $500,000 a year.

By 1779, as many as one in seven Americans in Washington's army was black.

Mary Ludwig Hays, nicknamed "Molly Pitcher," is arguably the most famous female who fought in the war. She replaced her wounded husband at his cannon during the Battle of Monmouth in 1778.

The Battle of Bunker Hill (1775) was actually fought on Breed's Hill. The confusion likely started after Abigail Adams witnessed fighting from her home in nearby Braintree and wrote to her husband that a friend of theirs had died at the battle of "Bunker Hill."

The term "Keep me posted" was coined during the Colonial Era. Long before the advent of Facebook and Twitter, people would tack a bit of news to a large wooden post to share information with the community.

American Settlers

🌿 Pioneers were the first people to settle in the frontiers of North America (from 1700 onward). They came from all walks of life. Many were farmers but some were doctors, shopkeepers, blacksmiths, missionaries, or lawyers, etc.

🌿 America really is the land of opportunity. One of the first things the pioneers did when they got to their new homes was buy land. At the time, land was priced at two dollars an acre.

🌿 The kitchen with its fireplace was the most important room in the house, but mainly because it was the only room in the house.

🌿 Randolph B. Marcy's *A Handbook for Overland Expeditions* was an essential manual for westward migration. First published in 1859, it contained practical advice on everything from route selection and wagon packing, to emergency medicine (for rattlesnake bites), and dealing with Native American people.

🌿 Early American pioneers felt that living in separate cabins did not protect them from the Native American people. Instead, settlers who lived near one another would inhabit a fort together.

A

🍂 Most people know Johnny Appleseed (given name John Chapman) was an American pioneer and missionary who planted apple seeds (hence the nickname) among other things. Most people don't know what *variety* of apple exactly. Turns out it's the same one that inspired novelist David Morell when choosing a name for his fictional hero—the "Rambo" apple with two varieties, one from Sweden and one from France.

🍂 Davy Crockett had a rifle named "Pretty Betsy." It followed one he called "Old Betsy."

🍂 The first person born in America to parents from England was named Virginia Dare. She was born in Roanoke Island (today part of North Carolina).

🍂 In the eighteenth century, Massachusetts sailors hunted whales. The oil from the marine mammals was used for soaps, perfumes, candles, and to light lamps.

🍂 By the second half of the eighteenth century, the English colonies were less than half English.

🍂 Seven mountains, eight streams, and ten lakes are named after America's first president, George Washington.

🍂 Marijuana was one of the crops grown on George Washington's farm.

American States

❧ Connecticut's name comes from an Algonquian word meaning "land on the long tidal river." The Nutmeg State is also known as the "Constitution State" and "Land of Steady Habits."

❧ Hawaii holds the record for the tallest sea cliffs in the world. Found in Kalaupapa (which was once a leper settlement), these cliffs can reach up to 3,300 feet (1,010 m).

❧ In Wisconsin, the National Mustard Museum boasts a collection of more than 5,000 jars, bottles, and tubes of prepared mustards from across the globe.

❧ Mississippi ranks as the most religious state in the U.S. According to a poll undertaken by Gallup in 2008 based on more than 350,000 interviews, 85 percent of Mississippians said "yes" when asked if religion was an important part of daily life.

❧ Florida supplies about 80 percent of America's demand for orange juice.

A

American Taxes

❧ In 2009, the IRS received a staggering 131,543,000 individual tax returns. If each return required one minute to process, it would still take 250 years for one taxman to complete the job.

❧ Word up … The Gettysburg Address has 269 words while the Declaration of Independence contains 1,337. The Holy Bible contains 773,000 words. The U.S. Tax Code puts them all to shame with over seven million words in total.

❧ Hand it over. In the state of Alabama, the government levied a 10-cent tax on the purchase of a deck of playing cards that contains "no more than 54 cards."

❧ Can it! Chicago has a fountain soda drink tax. If you purchase a fountain soda drink, you pay a nine percent tax. Buy the same drink in a bottle or a can and you only pay three percent.

❧ An unusual tax in Maine will have some people feeling blue. Anyone who grows, purchases, sells, handles, or processes blueberries in the state are subject to a three-fourths of a cent per pound tax.

❧ Maryland charges homeowners and businesses a tax on waste water. That's certainly one way to flush money down the toilet.

Ancient Egypt

◆ Rameses the Great (circa 1300–1213 B.C.E.) was rumored to have fathered more than 100 children.

◆ Rich Egyptians wore white, gauzy linens that were so light you could see right through them.

◆ Ancient Egyptians shaved their eyebrows to mourn cats that passed away. In many cases, the cats were mummified with elaborate wrappings and painted feline designs. There was a death sentence for causing a cat's death, deliberately or not.

◆ Hairstyling was important to ancient Egyptians, beginning in youth. Boys wore side ponytails with the rest of the hair shaved until the age of 12. Girls styled their hair into braids or ponytails. Males and females of all ages wore wigs for fancy occasions.

◆ As part of the mummy-making process, the intestines, liver, stomach, and lungs were removed and preserved separately. The heart stayed in the body and the brain was thrown out.

A

Animism

✦ The word "Animism" comes from the Latin word *anima*, meaning soul or breath. In describing African traditional religions, "Animism" is a shorthand term to describe a richer and more complex relationship between humans and nature spirits.

✦ The original religion of the African people was animism and many of the slaves brought to America were likely animists. Today 16 percent of Black Africans are Animists, 48 percent are Christians, and only 32 percent are Muslims.

✦ Head's up: the Jivaroan and Urarina tribe both practice the art of head shrinking. It is believed that if the spirit of one's mortal enemy is not trapped within the head, it can escape a slain body.

✦ In Animism, relationships are restored by sacrifice and appeasement, as opposed to repentance and forgiveness in religions like Christianity.

A

Apartheid

🍃 South Africa was colonized by the English and Dutch in the seventeenth century. An uneasy sharing of power between the two groups held sway until the 1940s, when the Afrikaner National Party was able to gain a strong majority. Strategists in the National Party invented apartheid (an odious system of legalized racial segregation) as a means to cement their control over the economic and social system.

🍃 Nelson Mandela's birth name *Rolihlahla* means "to pull a branch of a tree" or "troublemaker."

🍃 Apartheid depends upon the classification of people into separate racial categories. These determine where you can live, how much you are paid, and, until recently, whom you could sleep with. (Sexual relations between blacks and whites had been outlawed in South Africa's 1950 Immorality Act.)

🍃 The Land Act of 1913 passed by the newly allied Boers and British removed from black people the right to own land and apportioned 87 percent of South Africa's land to whites. It dictated that black and white communities should live in separate areas, travel in different buses, and stand in their own lines.

🍃 The country has 11 official languages. Nine are native African, one is English, and the last is Afrikaans, a language developed by the region's early Dutch settlers.

A

~ Today at the Apartheid Museum in Johannesburg, tickets are given out with the markers white and nonwhite to give visitors the experience of a divided state.

~ Nelson Mandela was one of 13 children.

~ In 2010 South Africa, which had for a long period been banned from international sports because of its policy of apartheid, became the first African nation to host the World Cup.

~ In 1997, South Africa's two anthems were combined into a single song. It is the world's only national anthem that begins and ends in different keys.

Archimedes

- Archimedes (287–212 B.C.E.) was a Greek mathematician, philosopher, and inventor who is most famous for discovering the law of hydrostatics, sometimes known as "Archimedes' principle." It stated that a body immersed in fluid loses weight equal to the weight of the amount of fluid it displaces.

- Paper had yet to be invented in Greece, so Archimedes used any surface he could to draw his figures, including writing in dust or ashes. Allegedly, he even drew figures on his body after bathing.

- Archimedes worked out Calculus 1,500 years before Newton and Leibniz.

- Archimedes approximated the number of grains of sand in the world to be 10 to the power of 63 (10^{63}). His account of the work that gave him this number is called *The Sand Reckoner.*

- The scientist was so excited about a discovery he once ran naked through the city streets. He had made a breakthrough in the public baths and needed to rush home to work out the solution.

- Archimedes was the son of Phidias the Astronomer. Apparently historians know only this single fact about the latter.

A

⤝ According to Plutarch, Archimedes was related to Hieron II, the king of Syracuse. After Syracuse was captured, Archimedes was killed by a Roman soldier. It is said that he was so absorbed in his calculations he told his killer not to disturb him.

⤝ The catapult and a rather ingenious system using a combination of mirrors to focus the sun's rays on invaders' boats and igniting them, are only two of the inventions attributed to Archimedes.

Architecture

❧ The first pyramid was the Step Pyramid at Saqqara, which was built for the Pharaoh Djoser (2630–2611 B.C.E.). It was designed by the architect Imhotep, who would eventually be regarded by the Egyptians as "The Father of Architecture, Sculpture, and Medicine."

❧ Early in the twelfth century, Gothic builders discovered that pointed arches could support more weight than perpendicular walls.

❧ There was no shortage of bizarre extravagance at the Palace of Versailles outside Paris. In 1685, 36,000 people and 6,000 horses were working on the palace, which measured 1,640 feet (500 m) in length and took 50 years to build. The chateau included a grand apartment, royal opera house, chapel, and an ornate hall of mirrors. And there was splendor in the grass ... the magnificent 250-acre (100-hectare) geometric garden is the quintessential formal French garden.

A

❧ The Chrysler Building in New York City was an Art Deco skyscraper designed by architect William Van Alen. It was the tallest building in the world for about a year (1930–1) until the Empire State Building was built.

❧ When colonizing North America, European settlers brought building influences from their own countries with them. The houses of the British settlers along the northeast coast are vastly different from the houses of the French in the Mississippi Valley and from the Spanish colonists in Florida and California.

Arctic Exploration

- Sought by explorers for centuries as a possible trade route, the Northwest Passage is a sea route through the Arctic Ocean, along the northern coast of North America connecting the Atlantic and Pacific Oceans.

- One of the most famous expeditions of the passage was made by Sir John Franklin who departed England in 1845 with two vessels and never returned. It was only 12 years later that some evidence was found, documenting that the vessels had been beset in ice for two years. Nobody survived the icy Arctic conditions.

- The Arctic is named for the north polar constellation "Arktos," which is Greek for "bear."

- The Arctic is 5.5 million square miles (14,245,000 square km)—almost exactly the same size as Antarctica—and has been inhabited by humans for close to 20,000 years.

- The Canadian Arctic is inhabited almost exclusively by Inuit. Their survival and economy is based on sea-mammal hunting.

- American explorers Frederick Cook and Robert Peary both claimed to have reached the North Pole, in 1908 and 1909 respectively. However, these may have been false claims as they may have turned back before actually getting to the pole. The first person to definitely achieve this feat was the American explorer Richard Byrd, who, with his copilot Floyd Bennett, flew over the pole in an aircraft on May 9, 1926.

A

✦ There were 52 sled dogs on the first Norwegian expedition to reach the South Pole in 1910.

✦ A 1744 act of British parliament offered money for the discovery of the Northwest Passage from the Atlantic Ocean to the Pacific Ocean. Only British subjects could be considered for an award. The British ship *Octavius* was the first voyage to attempt this mythical route, but the crew died during the winter of 1762, stuck in a sea ice bed without adequate supplies. During the next 13 years the boat made its way through the passage leading to the tabloid-like headline "Dead Men Discover Northwest Passage."

✦ On his final voyage Captain Cook's ship was thwarted by ice at 70 degrees 44 feet N.

✦ The Dutch explorer Willem Barents and his group took baths in wine barrels when they stayed on Novaya Zemlya, an archipelago in the Arctic Ocean. Although they endured the winter (the first Europeans to manage this feat) Barents himself did not survive to be rescued with the rest of his crew.

✦ An attempt by Lewis Gordon Pugh to kayak to the North Pole in 2008 was abandoned after three days. The British swimmer had achieved the feat of a one-kilometer (0.6-mile) North Pole swim the year before, a demonstration of how climate change had impacted the area.

Aristotle

🐦 At the age of 17, Aristotle (384–322 B.C.E.) joined Plato's (429–387 B.C.E.) Academy in Athens. Here, he studied science and philosophy for 20 years.

🐦 As well as a scientist, Aristotle was a man of the arts and culture. He wrote on a variety of subjects including poetry, music, theater, logic, metaphysics, rhetoric, ethics, and politics.

🐦 In his lifetime, Aristotle wrote as many as 200 treatises, but only 31 exist today.

🐦 Aristotle was 49 when he founded his own school in 335 B.C.E., the Lyceum, where philosophy, mathematics, and rhetoric were taught.

🐦 Sometime between 347 and 343 B.C.E., Aristotle settled in the city of Mytilene on the island of Lesbos. He spent much of this time dissecting fish.

A

Art

❧ The first Norman Rockwell (1894–1978) painting featured on the cover of the *Saturday Evening Post* depicted a group of kids mocking a boy pushing a baby carriage. It ran on May 20, 1916.

❧ Fifteenth-century artist, Italian Leon Battista Alberti (1404–1472) was also a physicist, philosopher, poet, and priest, among other occupations. One of his most impressive feats was hurling an apple over the highest rooftop in Genoa.

❧ Thirteenth-century artist Jao Tzu-jan specified Twelve Taboos in painting. Among them: "Roads Leading and Coming from Nowhere," "Figures Hunched," and "Buildings Jumbled Together."

❧ Thieves have taken Rembrandt's *Jacob III de Cheyn* four times and returned it anonymously in each case.

❧ Van Gogh completed approximately 900 paintings during his career. One sold in 1992 for $82.5 million. In his lifetime, however, he sold only one: *Red Vineyard at Arles.*

A

Australia

- You may want to jot this down: the Australians invented the notepad in 1902.

- In 1954, Bob Hawke secured a place in the *Guinness Book of Records* for downing a yard of ale (2.5 imperial pints or 1.4 liters) in 11 seconds. In 1984, he earned a place in parliament as the prime minister of Australia.

- On January 26, 1788, Captain Arthur Phillip founded Port Jackson and the first penal colony was born. This day is known as Australia Day.

- Australia is the world's smallest continent, but sixth-largest country.

- Azaria Chamberlain was a newborn who disappeared on a family camping trip in Ayers Rock in 1980. Her parents said she was snatched by a dingo, a kind of primitive, feral canine, giving rise to the sardonic saying "A dingo ate my baby." The baby's mother was convicted and later acquitted of her murder.

- From 1838 until 1902 it was not legal to swim during the day in Australia. Bathing was permitted at dawn and in the evening, but men and women had to remain separate.

- Australian women earned the right to vote in 1902. It was the second country to grant women's suffrage, after nearby New Zealand.

- Bees, moths, ants, and termites were all part of the Aborigines traditional diet.

✎ The band name "Three Dog Night" apparently came from a story written about Australian Aborigines that the lead singer's girlfriend had read. According to the article, on cold nights, the indigenous people would sleep with a dingo. A "three dog night" meant they were freezing.

Babylon

- Babylon was the capital of Babylonia. After the fall of the Assyrian Empire in 612 B.C.E., Babylon became the capital of the ancient Near East.

- Babylon was first mentioned in a dated tablet from the reign of Sargon of Akkad in 3,800 B.C.E.

- It was under the rule of King Nebuchadnezzar (605–562 B.C.E.) that Babylon became one of the most splendid cities of the ancient world. Nebuchadnezzar ordered the complete reconstruction of the imperial grounds, including the rebuilding of the Etemenanki and the construction of the Ishtar Gate, the most spectacular of eight gates that had ringed the perimeter of Babylon.

- One of the laws of the Code of Hammurabi, a set of laws formulated in ancient Babylon, stipulated that a man who owed money had the option of lending his wife out to work as a slave. Another set a fair, regulated price for beer.

- The Hanging Gardens of Babylon were built for the wife of Nebuchadnezzar II and were included in the first list of the Seven Wonders of the World.

Balkan Wars

🐦 Balkan Wars refers to the two wars that occurred in southeastern Europe in 1912 and 1913.

🐦 The first Balkan War began when the Balkan League—Serbia, Greece, Montenegro, and Bulgaria—launched a series of attacks on Turkey. Though they all had been part of the Turkish or Ottoman Empire at one time, Turkey was seen as weak and regarded as the "Sick Man of Europe."

🐦 Author B. Urlanis stated in *Voini I Narodo-Nacelenie Europi* that 122,000 people were killed in action, 20,000 died of wounds, and 82,000 died of disease in the first and second Balkan wars.

🐦 Greedy Bulgarians were unsatisfied with their gains from the peace settlement of the first war and launched the second Balkan War in 1913.

🐦 The first Balkan War ended on May 30, 1913, the same day that Igor Sikorsky became the first man to pilot a four-engine aircraft.

B

Bastille

- The Bastille was a fortress and state prison built in Paris after the Hundred Year's War (1337–1453) between the French and English.

- The *lettre de cachet* was a sealed document issued on behalf of the king. Such a letter could order imprisonment or exile of anyone without record to courts of law. Among the more prominent convicts of the late 1780s were Latude, a notorious and querulous swindler; the quack and alchemist Count Cagliostro; the diplomat and general Dumouriez; and the wallpaper manufacturer Reveillon.

- Life behind bars ... The Marquis de Sade (1740–1814) spent ten of his 32 years of incarceration in the Bastille.

- The medieval fortress was stormed by a horde of 8,000 men and women who were not there to liberate the prisoners, but to find the gunpowder and arms stored inside.

- Get shorty. On average standing 5 feet (1.5 m) tall, the people who stormed the Bastille were small in stature by today's standards.

- Bastille Day is a national holiday in France. It commemorates the storming of the Bastille on July 14, 1789, and celebrates the beginning of a new form of government.

Battle of Antietam

❧ The Battle of Antietam (1862), also known as the Battle of Sharpsburg, was the first major battle in the American Civil War to take place on Northern soil.

❧ The 12-hour battle commenced at 5:30 A.M. on September 17 and lasted until 5:30 P.M. that day.

❧ With about 23,000 casualties, Antietam earns the record for bloodiest single-day battle in American history.

❧ Robert E. Lee's Army of Northern Virginia had 45,000 troops battling against Union Army Major General George B. McClellan's 90,000.

B

❧ Nurse Clara Barton tended wounded soldiers and was so close to the battleground that a stray bullet went through her sleeve and killed a man she was treating.

Battle of Britain

🖎 In the summer of 1940, 2,936 pilots participated in the only battle in history to be fought entirely in the air. The war was against the German Luftwaffe.

🖎 1,389 German planes were lost while 792 British planes went down. When it became apparent that British air power was far superior to Germany's, Hitler called off the invasion.

B

🖎 The British success was due in part to a chain of new radar stations, which gave advanced warning of approaching attackers.

🖎 After the battle, the Air Ministry published a 32-page publicity pamphlet documenting the air raid in 1941. More than a million copies were sold in Britain alone.

Battle of Hastings, The

❧ The Battle of Hastings was fought between the Norman army of Duke William II of Normandy (circa 1028–1087) and the English army of King Harold II (circa 1022–1066). The battle began at 9 A.M. on October 14, 1066, and was decisively won nine hours later by the Normans.

❧ King Harold II was believed to have been shot in the eye with an arrow. A plaque located in Battle, East Sussex, marks the place where he is thought to have fallen.

❧ The so-called Bayeux Tapestry depicts the events before, during, and after the Battle of Hastings on a piece of fabric 230-feet (70-m) long. It is displayed and preserved in Bayeux in Normandy, in northern France, though very little is known about its origin.

B

❧ The Battle of Hastings is an example of the application of combined-arms warfare. The Norman bowmen, cavalry, and infantry teamed up to put the English in a vulnerable defensive position.

❧ William the Conqueror was originally called William the Bastard. His father (1000–1035) had been called "Robert the Devil."

❧ In eleventh-century England, the earls had more authority than the king.

❧ William the Conqueror's body would not fit into his coffin. He was too large for it and his body had become even more bloated after his death because of the heat. King Philip of France had once described William as having the appearance of a pregnant woman.

❧ On April 26, 1066, Halley's Comet was seen in England and was generally regarded as a bad omen.

Battle of the Bulge, The

❧ The Battle of the Bulge was fought during the brutal months of 1944–45 as the Nazi's last major offensive against the Allies in World War II.

❧ President Eisenhower (1890–1969) spread the U.S. army over a 600-mile (965-km) front, but failed to provide enough defense in the Ardennes toward Antwerp. Consequently, the Germans broke through the American lines and advanced 60 miles (96 km), causing the "bulge."

❧ Hitler lost 250,000 men and 600 tanks during this attack, without any backup left.

❧ One of the weapons used by German soldiers was an MG 42 machine gun. It boasted a rate of fire of 1,200rpm. More than 750,000 were manufactured in 1945.

❧ Many American soldiers were killed on surrendering.

❧ In poor weather conditions, the GI rifles would sometimes freeze and only urinating on them in action could unjam them.

B

Bay of Pigs

❧ In an attempt to overthrow the Cuban premier Fidel Castro, the United States launched an unsuccessful attack on Cuba. Though 1,300 exiles armed with U.S. weapons landed at Bahia de Cochinos (Bay of Pigs), the operation was so poorly planned Castro's forces quickly defeated them.

❧ Four American pilots were killed in battle and 1,189 were taken prisoner.

❧ Most prisoners were released to the U.S. within a year in exchange for $53 million in food and medicine.

❧ After the rather embarrassing attack, President Kennedy fired long-time CIA Director Allen W. Dulles, Deputy Director Charles P. Cabell, and Deputy Director Richard Bissell.

❧ The Canadian indie-rock band Destroyer released "Bay of Pigs" in 2009, a 13.5-minute disco track about the invasion.

B

Berlin Wall

🐦 Checkpoint Charlie—a border checkpoint that opened ten days after East Berlin was sealed off—was accessible to foreign tourists, military from the Western powers, and diplomats. A sign at Checkpoint Charlie that reads, "You are leaving the American Sector" in English, Russian, French, and German still exists at the point, alongside a security hut and surrounding sandbags.

🐦 The Berlin Wall spanned nearly 100 miles (about 160 km) with a second fence built 300 feet (90 m) in front of it. The area between the fence and the wall was a barren no-man's land known as the "death strip."

🐦 The great escape? Between 1961 and 1989, approximately 5,000 people managed to escape across the Wall and into West Berlin but more than 136 people—mostly young men between the ages 16 and 30—were shot and killed at the wall. An additional 251 people died during regular border crossings, mainly from heart attacks.

🐦 Escape was only bound by the imagination. Original escapes ranged from tunneling, to driving a short car underneath a gate, to creating small ultralights and flying across. Desperate times call for desperate measures.

🐦 Only a little bit of the Berlin Wall remains today—not even the watchtowers that stood in East Berlin are still standing.

B

Black Death

 The Black Death was a plague that killed off approximately 75,000,000 people from 1347 to 1351. That was one-third to one-half of the European population.

 Flea-infested rats caused the outbreak. The fleas carried a bacterium called *Yersinia pestis,* which caused three types of the plague.

 The three forms of the plague were bubonic, pneumonic, and septicemic, which all attacked the body's lymphatic system. Symptoms included enlargement of the glands, high fevers, headaches, vomiting, and extremely painful joints.

B The septicemic form caused the skin to turn purple because, with this form of plague, all of the cells in the body hemorrhaged.

 There was an outbreak of plague as recently as 1924. It struck in Los Angeles and resulted in 33 deaths.

Black Panthers

🐦 When Jamaican-born Marcus Garvey (1887–1940) moved to New York in 1916, he observed there was little hope for black people to enjoy full civil rights and equality in the near future. As a result, his belief in black nationalism, black pride, and racial separation made him a forerunner of the Black Nationalism of Malcolm X and the Black Panthers.

🐦 Huey Newton, Leroy Eldridge Cleaver, and Bobby Searle created The Black Panther Party for Self Defense as a measure to protect black people from police brutality.

🐦 By 1985, the Panthers had ceased to exist as an organized party.

🐦 The fictional comic book character Black Panther, first appearing in *Fantastic Four*, in issue 52, published in July 1966, pre-dates the Black Panther Party by three months. The comic sold for 12 cents.

🐦 At the 1968 Summer Olympics, Tommie Smith and John Carlos, the American gold and bronze medalists in the 200m, gave the Black Power salute during the playing of the national anthem during the ceremony when they were presented with their medals.

B

Blizzard of 1888

❧ The big chill. A blizzard ravaged the northeastern United States as well as the Atlantic provinces of Canada between March 11 and 14 in 1888. "The Great White Hurricane" paralyzed most of the area, taking more than 400 lives, about half of them in New York City alone.

❧ Fifty inches (1.3 m) of snow fell in Connecticut and Massachusetts, while New Jersey and New York State had 40 inches (1 m). Snow drifts towering at 50ft (15 m) buried houses and trains.

❧ The New York Historical Society's reference library showcases an exhibition on the blizzard and includes photographs, half letters, newspapers, and other memorabilia of the town's snow-in.

B

❧ Theodore Roosevelt (1858–1919), who lived in the East 60s, trudged through the blizzard to keep an appointment with the librarian of the New York Historical Society, which was fifty blocks away. He arrived to discover the librarian had not shown up and walked back home. In a laconic letter, he wrote to her, "I presume the blizzard kept you at home."

❧ To qualify as a blizzard, a storm must meet these extremes: snow; wind blowing at 35 mph (55 km/h) for at least three hours; 10° F (-12°C); and visibility of no greater than 1,500 feet (460 m).

❧ Fifteen thousand subway passengers were trapped on New York City's elevated railroad. The fare for the train was 5 cents. Some men provided ladders to help them escape, charging passengers $2 for a one-way trip.

🕊 A writer at New York's *Evening Sun* noted that sparrows were unable to fly against the wind in the blizzard.

🕊 The weather in the region was unusually warm in the days before the blizzard struck.

🕊 At one point during the storm people were able to "walk on water" from Brooklyn to Manhattan because of the thick layer of ice on the East River.

Bohemia

- Bohemia is a historical region in central Europe, which comprises of the western two-thirds of the traditional Czech lands.

- Bohemia started out as a duchy in the ninth century and flourished into a kingdom by 1198.

- The name Bohemia comes from the Celtic Boii tribe, who inhabited the region from around the fourth century B.C.E.

- St. Wenceslas, the patron saint of Bohemia, was executed under the orders of his younger brother, Boleslav, who took over the Bohemian throne.

- Wazzzup ... Two of America's most beloved beers hail from Bohemia: Budweiser originated in the city of Budweis and Pilsner came from the town Plzen.

B

Boleyn, Anne

🐦 Dark skinned, dark eyed, and dark haired, Anne Boleyn (circa 1501–1536), the second wife of King Henry VIII (1491–1547) was the complete opposite of the conventional Tudor beauty of the time. Allegedly, a sixth finger grew from her pinkie and she had a large mole on her neck.

🐦 A charmed life. Anne was often described as witty, intelligent, proud, brave, quick-tempered, stubborn, ambitious, and haughty.

🐦 She was responsible for telling King Henry that the Bible should be translated into English and made available to everyone, not just the clergy.

🐦 Catherine of Aragon, King Henry VIII's first wife was so well favored by the public that when Anne became Henry's second wife, hatred and jealousy for the Boleyn family escalated. Ms. Boleyn was often called a "witch" and "the whore."

🐦 Anne was a talented musician who played several instruments including the lute, harp, and virginal. She also had a lovely singing voice.

🐦 Off with her head! In court, Anne admitted that her marriage was not legal to ensure an execution by beheading. Why? King Henry had ordered her execution and she was petrified of the other option—death by burning.

B

Bolívar, Simón

❧ Simón Bolívar (1783–1830) was a Venezuelan military and political leader who played a vital role in leading Bolivia, Colombia, Ecuador, Panama, Peru, and Venezuela in the fight for independence from the Spanish Empire (1819).

❧ The founding father's full name was Simón José Antonio de la Santísima Trinidad Bolívar y Palacios, and he was often regarded as the "George Washington of South America."

❧ Bolívar had such admiration for Thomas Jefferson (1743–1826) that he sent his nephew to the University of Virginia, which was founded and designed by Jefferson, a former American president.

B

❧ Bolivia and Venezuela (the Bolivarian Republic of Venezuela) are both named after Bolívar.

❧ Bolívar personally drafted the Bolivian Constitution of 1826.

❧ In 1999 Venezuela was officially renamed the Bolivarian Republic of Venezuela, after the revolutionary leader who played a major role in liberating the country from colonization.

◗ Venezuelan president, Hugo Chavez, oversaw the exhumation of Simon Bolívar's remains in July of 2010 with the ostensible purpose of discovering whether the hero had been poisoned rather than having died of tuberculosis, as recorded in the history books. Scientists have indeed claimed that it is likely Bolívar ingested arsenic, however, they are fairly certain that it was unintentionally consumed through drinking contaminated water during his time in Peru, rather than an assassination attempt by an adversary.

◗ According to an account given by Ducoudray Holstein, El Libertador, as Bolívar was also known, was 5 foot 4 inches (1.6 m) tall.

◗ Bolívar was only 19 years old when his wife died.

Bolsheviks

- *Bolshevik* is the Russian word for majority. The Bolshevik Party, founded in 1903 by Vladimir Lenin (1870–1924), was an organized mass revolutionary party comprised of the Russian working class, which sought to overthrow the Czar through revolution.

- The Bolshevik Party was born out of Russia's Social Democrat Party. When the party split in 1903, the Bolsheviks only had one obvious leader— Vladimir Lenin.

- Red alert! During the days of the Cold War, Labour union leaders and other left wingers in the United Kingdom were occasionally described as "Bolshie" while the equivalent terms "Commie," "Red," or "Pinko" were used in the U.S.

- George Orwell's dystopic novel *Animal Farm* is an allegory of the Bolshevik revolution.

B

Boston Tea Party

 When the parliament of Great Britain passed the Tea Act in 1773, it allowed the East India Company to ship tea directly to North America. This eliminated British and American middleman and reduced import tax. Americans could now purchase cheaper tea directly, but this enraged merchants, who had been smuggling Dutch tea into the colonies for several years and considered this act a conspiracy to eliminate them as middlemen.

 On December 16, 1773, several hundred Bostonians—mostly young apprentices and artisans in training—put on face paint and Indian headdresses, and then dumped 324 chests of tea belonging to the East India Company to the bottom of the harbor.

 Thoroughly disgusted with the colonists, the Parliament passed the Coercive Acts, which closed the port of Boston to all shipping until the colony paid for the destroyed tea.

 Tea ... for two? Many of us have heard the story of the group of colonists who destroyed the tea by throwing it into Boston Harbor on December 16, 1773, but very few realize that there was a repeat performance on March 7, 1774. The two tea parties cost the British the equivalent of $3 million today.

B

Brazil

❧ October 12, 1931, the 98-foot (30-m) statue of Christ the Redeemer in Rio de Janeiro was unveiled on the top of Corcovado Mountain as a Brazilian monument to 100 years of independence from Portugal.

❧ Before the arrival of the Portuguese colonizers (1500s), Brazil was inhabited by indigenous Indian tribes, with their own distinct animist cults and mythology.

❧ The Portuguese settlers frequently intermarried with both the Indians and the African slaves, and there were also mixed marriages between the Africans and Indians.

B

❧ In the nineteenth century, coffee took the place of sugar as Brazil's most important product.

❧ There is a line of "coffee presidents" in Brazil, so named for their close ties to the coffee industry.

❧ Brazil has won the World Cup four times—more often than any other country.

❧ Explorer Pedro Álvares Cabral (circa 1467–1520) was actually looking for Asia when he stumbled upon the land known today as Brazil.

❧ In the 1960s the capital was moved from Rio to Brasilia in an effort to put an end to the country's obsession with the coastline and beaches. The plan failed.

🦢 As of 2001, Brazil had 18,578 miles (30,000 km) of railroad tracks.

🦢 The Amazon is 4,000 miles (about 6,500 km) long, but what's more surprising is its width. At certain points you cannot see the shore from a riverboat riding down the center of the river.

🦢 Sao Paulo, the biggest city in Brazil, is 47 miles (75 km) inland.

Buddhism

⁓ By finding the path to enlightenment, Siddhartha Gautama found the religion of Buddhism, a 2,500-year-old religion with a focus on personal, spiritual development.

⁓ According to ancient Buddhist law, it's okay to eat an animal if you were a witness to it being killed, as long as it wasn't killed for you.

B

⁓ It was a banker who built the first Buddhist monastery.

⁓ The Bodhi tree, a swastika (considered a symbol of good luck in India), a wheel, and a footprint were all used as symbols for the Buddha before the first century C.E.

⁓ A Mongol leader Altan Khan gave the title "Dalai Lama" to Buddhist leaders in 1578.

⁓ It took 12 years and 130,000 wood blocks to make the first printed Buddhist canon.

Caligula

🌿 Caligula (12–41 C.E.), was a depraved despot who thought he really was a god. According to biographer Suetonius, while Caligula was emperor of the Roman Empire (37–41 C.E.), he dressed as the Roman God Jupiter, wore a golden beard, and a thunderbolt, and stood at a temple like a statue to be worshipped.

🌿 As a ruthless and cruel autocrat, Caligula devised new methods of torture such as covering the victim with honey and letting loose a swarm of wasps.

🌿 Cut! Bob Guccione, founder of the lad's mag *Penthouse*, produced and financed the 1979 movie *Caligula* starring Malcolm McDowell as Caligula. As Bob felt the movie didn't contain enough sex, he secretly filmed real sex scenes performed by porn stars and added them to the final edit. The movie was banned in the UK for nearly 30 years.

🌿 Caligula had incestuous relationships with his sisters as well as anyone of either sex who caught his eye.

🌿 On January 24, 41 C.E., two guards fatally stabbed Caligula in the genitals after he had humiliated them. Not satisfied with Caligula's death, the guards also killed his wife and baby daughter.

🌿 When he finally became emperor, Caligula had his horse Incitatus made a consul in the Roman senate.

Caliphs

~🐦 The term caliph—the name given to a leader of a Muslim community—comes from the Arabic word "khalifa" which is short for *Khalifa-tu-Rasulillah*, "successor to the Messenger of God."

~🐦 The main caliphs following the Prophet Muhammad's death were Caliph Abu Bakr, Omar, Uthman, and Ali—all known as the Rightly Guided Caliphs of Islam.

~🐦 During Muhammad's final hours, Abu Bakr led the community in prayer and it was understood that he would succeed Muhammad as the future leader.

C
~🐦 Some detractors considered Abu Bakr—a wealthy merchant who grew up together with Muhammad—to be too soft and emotional to be a prominent leader.

~🐦 Caliph Uthman, who was married to Muhammad's daughter Ruqaiyah, led the efforts to preserve the Qur'an and to this day, it remains in its original form.

~🐦 In 656 C.E. Uthman, the third caliph, was assassinated in his home by a group of Egyptians.

Calvinism

🐦 Calvinism, a form of Protestantism, was based on a theology created by a young Frenchman named John Calvin (1509–1564). In essence, he believed in absolute depravity of man after the fall of Adam and the impossibility of salvation with the exception of the very few—the Elect—who were predestined by God to salvation.

🐦 In 1541, Calvin settled in Geneva, a theocratic state that was self-governed by the believers.

🐦 Calvin banned swearing, gambling, and fornication. Skipping a church service was met with punishment. Adulterous women were drowned and men were beheaded, but the most severe punishments were reserved for heretics, who were burnt.

C

🐦 In Calvinism, religious conversations were encouraged and excessive drinking, indecent songs, cursing, games involving cards or dice, and dancing were forbidden. In fact, Calvin and his followers used to campaign against the social elite who danced at weddings.

🐦 Contrary to his image as an unyielding religious tyrant, Calvin enjoyed some of life's greatest pleasures including fine wine and long conversations with friends over dinner.

Cape Verde

- Cape Verde is an island country located off the western coast of Africa, opposite Mauritania and Senegal.

- Cape Verde is a mestizo society: 78 percent Creole, 28 percent black African, and one percent white.

- It is considered rude to eat in the company of others without sharing, so people on Cape Verde refrain from eating in public, such as on the street or on a bus.

- The national dish, *cachupa*, is a stew made with hominy, beans, and meat or vegetables. The popular drink *grog*, or sugar cane liquor, is manufactured on the islands and enjoyed, particularly by men, in the country.

- When someone passes away in Cape Verde, family members must dress in black for a full year after the death and are not allowed to play music or dance.

- American brand names that are popular among African-Americans are most highly regarded in Cape Verde.

C

Capitalism

❧ According to a 2009 poll by the BBC World Service, just 11 percent of people from 27 countries thought that free-market capitalism works well.

❧ From 1950 to 1963 in the United States, individuals earning above $200,000 had to pay 91 percent or 92 percent of their income to the federal government.

❧ Around the time of the 2008 Presidential election, 37 percent of young people in the U.S. preferred capitalism to socialism.

❧ Michael Moore's Detroit premier for his movie *Capitalism: A Love Story* was held at a movie theater located in the same building as the General Motors Headquarters. He was only allowed entrance without any cameramen or members of the press.

C

Carter, Jimmy

❧ James Earl Carter (born 1924), America's thirty-ninth President, is a life-long tennis player. We imagine he makes quite a racket on the court.

❧ He shot his sister Gloria in the rear with a BB gun after she threw a wrench at him. Consequently, his father punished him.

❧ He was denied the honor of being high school class Valedictorian because he skipped school to go to a movie. Hopefully, the title of President of the United States made up for it.

❧ His first car was a 1948 Studebaker "Commander."

C   ❧ When it comes to the environment and minimizing the use of natural resources, Jimmy Carter was well ahead of his time. He sought alternative fuel systems and insisted that American car manufacturers design more fuel-efficient cars. When Reagan came to power, he reversed most of Carter's proposal for conservation and alternative energy policies.

❧ Jimmy Carter said, "America did not invent human rights. In a very real sense human rights invented America."

Castles

🐦 Located in Bavaria, the Neuschwanstein Castle was built in the nineteenth century for King Ludwig II. Though it looks like a medieval castle from the outside, it was quite modern, with state-of-the-art technology at the time. Each floor had toilets with an automatic flushing system and there was an air-heating system for the entire castle.

🐦 Chillingham Castle, a twelfth-century building in Northumberland is Britain's most haunted castle. Allegedly, a "blue boy" haunts the Pink Room. Guests have reported seeing blue flashes of light above their bed after a long loud wailing.

🐦 Cinderella Castle at Walt Disney World, Orlando, Florida is 189-feet (57-m) tall and made out of fiberglass.

🐦 Built in the sixteenth-century, Predjamski castle located near Postojna, Slovenia, was the home of a renowned robber baron, Knight Erazem Lueger. More interesting is the fact that part of the castle was constructed within a cave.

🐦 Most of the castles William the Conquerer (circa 1028–1087) built were made of wood.

🐦 Lawrence of Arabia (1888–1935) liked to draw castles as he rode through the French countryside as a boy.

🐦 Breakfast served in medieval castles was usually bread and ale.

C

🖎 Bathrooms were called "garderobes" and hay was used for toilet paper.

🖎 A "license to crenellate" was necessary to construct a medieval castle in some countries (crenellation being the right to fortify and build embattlements).

🖎 Staircases generally spiraled to the right so that a right-handed defender could easily swing his sword as he backed up the staircase. This way the invader would have to twist his body around to try to reach his opponent.

Catherine de Medici

❧ Catherine de Medici (1519–1589) was the queen of France for 12 years, and queen mother for 30 years. Her three sons—Francis II (who ruled for one year from 1559–1560 and was married to Mary, Queen of Scots)—Charles IX (1560–1574), and Henry III (1574–1589)—may have reigned over France, but that period is often called "the age of Catherine de Medici" such was the influence of the mother over her sons.

❧ Catherine took ten years to conceive her first child (though she did get married at 14) and it is claimed she was given pills of myrrh to help bring on her puberty and enable her to conceive. It is also cited that Catherine tried every known treatment for getting pregnant, such as placing cow dung and ground stags' antlers on her "source of life," and drinking mule's urine.

❧ In a dream, Catherine had predicted the death of her husband (Henry II of France) in a dream in which she saw him being pierced in the eye by a lance during a jousting tournament. In actual fact Henry did meet his maker during a jousting tournament when the lance split and one bit entered his eye and another, his throat. From that day, Catherine took a broken lance as her emblem, inscribed with the words "*lacrymae hinc, hinc dolor*" ("from this come my tears and my pain"), and wore black in memory of Henry.

❧ Catherine was also a firm believer in astrology and her astrologer Luc Gauric also predicted the king's death in a joust.

C

🌿 There is speculation that Catherine de Medici disliked her daughter-in-law Mary Stuart (Mary, Queen of Scots) so much that she poisoned her own son Francis in order to bring an end to Mary's reign as the Queen of France. Catherine is similarly accused of murdering her son-in-law's mother, Jeanne d'Albret, shortly before her daughter Marguerite's wedding to Henry of Bourbon. Huguenot writers claim that she did so by giving Jeanne a gift of poisoned gloves.

🌿 Marriage did not suit Catherine's daughter Marguerite, and she soon took up a string of lovers. Catherine insisted that Henry get his wife under control. Henry locked Marguerite away in the Chateau d'Usson while he had one of her lovers (a man by the name of d'Aubiac) executed. He did not, however, carry out the deed in front of Marguerite, as Catherine had insisted.

Catherine of Aragon

❧ Catherine (1458–1536) was petite with long, golden-auburn hair, wide blue eyes, a round face, and a fair complexion.

❧ A Spanish princess, Catherine was first sent off to England in 1501 to marry Prince Arthur, but when he died less than a year into their marriage, Catherine married his brother, Henry VIII.

❧ Henry and Catherine were married for almost 20 years and had six children, though only one survived. Desperate for a male heir, Henry asked the Pope to annul their marriage as he thought that lack of an heir was God's punishment for marrying his brother's widow.

❧ Catherine died on January 7, 1536, at the age of 50, at Kimbolton Castle, in Peterborough, England. The castle is now a boarding school.

C

❧ Catherine's heraldic badge was a crowned pomegranate, a fruit of her labor so to speak.

Catherine the Great

- The Russian empress Catherine II, better known as Catherine the Great (1729–1796), reigned from 1762–1796.

- During her reign, she expanded the Russian Empire, improved administration, and energetically pursued the policy of Westernization.

- Catherine was known to have said, "I praise loudly, I blame softly."

- According to Michael Farquhar, author of *A Treasury of Royal Scandals*, she was a powerful woman with a promiscuous sex life, and she once had a lover 40 years her junior.

- Catherine's husband, Karl Ulrich (1728–1762), was believed to be impotent.

- Catherine's given name was actually Sophia.

- The poem "Waterfall" by Gavriil Romanovich Derzhavin was written about one of Catherine's lovers, Prince Potemkin.

- Catherine renounced the title "Catherine the Great," preferring history to form its own opinion of what she contributed to Russia, her adopted homeland (she was born in Pomerania).

- Catherine the Great died of a stroke while sitting on the commode in the palace at St. Petersburg.

Charlemagne

❧ Charlemagne (742–814), was king of the Franks and emperor of the West. He was also known as Carolus Magnus, Charles the Great, and Charles I. Carolus Magnus stood for Charles the Big (as well as Charles the Great), a contrast to his father, "Pippin the Short."

❧ The king was surprised when he was given so much responsibility at his coronation, which took place on Christmas Day in the year 800. He had thought his son would rule over the Franks and Lombards. In fact, Charlemagne possessed the largest territory to be governed under one ruler in Europe in the Middle Ages.

❧ Charlemagne made celibacy compulsory among the priests of the lands he conquered.

C

❧ Charlemagne was married five times and had many children, but only one—Louis the Debonair—was legitimate. He became Louis I, inheritor of his father's empire.

❧ In a deck of playing cards, the King of Hearts represents Charlemagne.

❧ Charlemagne reorganized the monetary system, devising the system of pounds, shillings, and pence, which had been used throughout Europe in the Middle Ages and in Britain until the 1970s.

❧ He had a palace and a cathedral built in his favorite town, *Aachen* (or Aix-la-Chapelle), where he also died and was buried.

❧ The peacock was first served as food during his reign.

Cherokee

❧ The word "Cherokee" is derived from the Choctaw word *Cha-la-kee*, which translates as "those who live in the mountains" or "those who live in the caves." The Cherokees originally named themselves *Ah-ni-yv-wi-ya*, meaning "these are all the human people."

❧ Depp thoughts … Johnny Depp's great-grandmother Minnie was full-blooded Cherokee.

❧ Warriors of AniKituhwa, a dance group who perform traditional Cherokee war dances, are the official cultural ambassadors by the Tribal Council of the Eastern Band of Cherokee. Dances include the Eagle Tail Dance, Bear Dance, Beaver Hunting Dance, and Friendship Dance.

❧ Good hair … The Long Hair Clan donned elaborate hairdos with waves, and curls. They wove various items into their hair as dramatic accents.

❧ Unlike the Woodland or Plains people, Cherokee only wore feathers in time of war or while playing a ball game, which was similar to lacrosse.

❧ The women wore short tunics made of deerskin, which were belted at the waist with woven belts, and accentuated with bone pins or carved brooches. They looked fabulous!

C

◦ The Trail of Tears is used to describe the exiling of Cherokee from their ancestral home in the southeast to Oklahoma. Fifteen to twenty thousand Cherokee Indians, along with other tribes, were herded off of their land and forced on an 800-mile (1,300-km) march that left many dead from exposure, starvation, disease, and exhaustion

◦ Cherokee women, who discovered how to grow corn, were accredited for the invention of agriculture. The Cherokee name for corn is *Selu*, the same name of the first woman in Cherokee mythology.

◦ As a young bride, Nancy Ward (circa 1738–1822), accompanied her husband in the battle with the Creeks and led the Cherokee to victory. As an outspoken advocate of peace, she was also known as the "Beloved Woman," who often acted as a mediator between the indigenous people and the white settlers.

◦ 22,000 people speak Cherokee today.

Children at War

❧ It is estimated that there are currently 300,000 children under 18 fighting in wars around the world.

❧ Bugler John Cook (1847–1915) was just 15 years old when he served in the U.S. Army and received the Medal of Honor for his acts during the Battle of Antietam in the Civil War.

❧ Double trouble ... Twin brothers Johnny and Luther Htoo were leaders of a rebel group known as God's Army, which was opposed to the Burmese military government. They were just 12 years old when they held hundreds of people hostage at Ratchaburi, a Thai hospital in the year 2000.

❧ In the past decade, it is estimated that more than 2 million children have been killed and more than 10 million injured or disabled in armed conflicts.

❧ Celebrated worldwide on February 12, Red Hand Day is an annual commemoration day to draw awareness to the practice of using children as soldiers in wars and armed conflicts.

C

Christ, Jesus

🥄 Jesus Christ was born in about 4 B.C.E. in Palestine and was crucified by the Roman Governor of Palestine in about 30 C.E.

🥄 A sixth-century mosaic in Ravenna, Italy, depicts JC wearing a purple royal toga with a gold stripe on his tunic. Christ was not a Roman citizen, however, so he would not have been entitled to wear a toga. As a Jewish man, Jesus would have been bearded but the mosaic shows him to be clean-shaven.

C

🥄 The name Jesus is ranked sixty-fifth in popularity for males of all ages in a sample of 2000–2003 Social Security Administration statistics.

🥄 Martin Scorsese's movie *The Last Temptation of Christ* attracted plenty of controversy because of a sex scene between Jesus (Willem Dafoe) and Mary Magdalene (Barbara Hershey). French zealots in Paris launched Molotov cocktails at a theater as a protest against the movie and injured 13 people. *Mon dieu!*

Christianity

❧ Christianity is the main religion of Africa with approximately 350 million worshippers. This trumps the number of followers in North America, which is 250 million.

❧ Christians believe that the main causes of cruelty are avarice, contempt for nature, and unkindness.

❧ Predating the New Testament, the Didache (pronounced *"did* ah kay") is a short Christian treatise that provides details regarding baptism, Eucharist, and church leadership.

❧ Though the Bible is the bestselling book of all time, it does not appear on *The New York Times* bestseller list because the list ranks the rate of sales of a title in a week at selected stores across the country.

❧ Christian missionaries arrived in Japan more than 450 years ago and won hundreds of thousands of converts. This prompted the Japanese shogun to launch a severe crackdown on the religion, which was banned in 1626 for nearly 250 years.

C

Civil Rights Movement

🐦 In the 1950s in the U.S., many states banned Black Americans from voting, attending "white" schools, dining in "white" restaurants, or joining unions. In 1947 President Truman (1884–1972) proposed a law to end such discrimination, but the U.S. congress rejected the proposal.

🐦 In 1954, the U.S. Supreme Court declared that school segregation was unconstitutional.

🐦 On October 1, 1962, two people were killed and at least 75 injured in a riot at the University of Mississippi, spurred by the attendance of the school's first black student, James Meredith. President Kennedy sent federal troops to quell the riots.

C

🐦 Bayard Rustin was one of the most prominent leaders of the Civil Rights movement, but his name was seldom mentioned in the press or media due in some part to the fact that he was openly gay.

🐦 Martin Luther King Jr. Day was established as a federal holiday in 1983 on the third Monday of January each year.

Cleopatra

🐦 Cleopatra was 17 years old when she took to the throne of Egypt in 51 B.C.E.

🐦 Cleopatra was well educated, spoke nine languages, and was the first of her family to speak Egyptian.

🐦 She married her brother Ptolemy XIII who was five years her junior. At the time, it was customary for brother and sister to marry and rule jointly.

🐦 Cleo wasn't the easiest on the eyes. According to historians, she was short and portly with a long hooked nose and a thick neck.

🐦 The budget for Elizabeth Taylor's costumes in the 1963 movie *Cleopatra* was the highest ever for an actor at the time. Her 65 dresses amounted to $194,800 and included a dress made from 24-carat gold cloth.

C

Clinton, Bill

❧ Bill Clinton was born as William Jefferson Blythe III on August 19, 1946, in Hope, Arkansas.

❧ His father, a traveling salesman, died in a car accident three months before he was born and Bill took on the name of his stepfather.

❧ In 1978, he became the youngest governor of the state of Arkansas. He was 32 at the time.

❧ During Clinton's term, unemployment dropped by half to four percent, the lowest in 40 years, while a rise in economic activity led to the introduction of 15 million new jobs.

❧ He is quoted as saying, "There is nothing wrong in America that can't be fixed with what is right in America."

C

Code of Hammurabi

❧ Dating back to 1750 B.C.E., the ancient Babylonian Code of Hammurabi is the oldest known code of laws. It was carved on a black stone monument, in 3,600 lines of cuneiform (one of the earliest writing systems devised), and stands 8 feet (2.4 m) tall. It currently resides at the Louvre Museum in Paris

❧ One law stipulated that if a husband divorces his wife, he must also return her dowry. A divorced woman also retained custody of any children.

❧ Another law stated that if a wife was caught committing adultery with another man, both had to be tied and thrown into water to drown.

❧ If a "sister of a god," or nun, entered a tavern to drink, she would be burned to death.

C

❧ One hand doesn't always know what the other is doing? If a son struck his father, his hands would be cut off as punishment.

Cold War

- The Cold War was an ideological battle between the U.S. and Western Europe, which championed capitalism versus the former USSR and Eastern Europe, which were communist. It lasted from 1945–1990.

- May the force be with you ... President Ronald Reagan (1911–2004) called the USSR "the evil empire," a term he picked up from the movie *Star Wars*.

- Before filming his 1964 movie *Dr. Strangelove*, a black comedy about nuclear war, director Stanley Kubrick (1928–1999) read nearly 50 books on the subject as research.

- The Cold War cost the U.S. eight trillion dollars in military expenditures and more than 100,000 lives lost in Korea and Vietnam.

- *Black Widow: The Coldest War* is a graphic novel published by Marvel. Set in the last days of the war, the main character, known as the Black Widow, works as a Russian agent who falls for American superheroes. When she eventually defects to the West in the story, she becomes an agent of S.H.I.E.L.D. and an occasional leader.

C

Communism

🐚 Italian dictator Benito Mussolini (1883–1945), the son of a blacksmith, was a communist until his experience of World War I, which convinced him to change his ideology to fascism.

🐚 In 1921, six million people died from famine in Russia as a result of the policies of the communist government led by Vladimir Lenin (1870–1924), which took complete control of all businesses in the country, including food distribution.

🐚 FBI chief J. Edgar Hoover (1895–1972) accused silent movie star Charlie Chaplin (1889–1977) of incorporating communist propaganda into his movies. However, the government had little evidence to prove Chaplin was any threat to national security.

🐚 Is there a Red under your Bed? Senator McCarthy (1908–1957) was a right-wing Republican who fueled widespread fear of communist subversion. He subpoenaed some of the most prominent entertainers at the time including Orson Welles, Lucille Ball, Dashiell Hammett, Leonard Bernstein, and Arthur Miller for questioning.

🐚 Mao Tse-Tung is quoted as saying, "Politics is war without bloodshed while war is politics with bloodshed."

C

Congo

~✿ French is the official language of the Congo.

~✿ Approximately 70 percent of the men and 44 percent of the women are literate.

~✿ The Democratic Republic of Congo gained independence from Belgium in 1960 but suffered from political turmoil and corruption.

~✿ In the late nineteenth century, King Leopold II (1835–1909), a heinous Belgian tyrant, transformed the country into a mass labor camp, amassed fortunes from the rubber trees, and massacred 10 million Africans in the Congo.

~✿ A yellow band divides the flag diagonally. The upper triangle is green and the lower is red. The green represents agriculture and forest, the yellow symbolizes friendship and nobility, and the red has been associated with the struggle for independence.

Conquistadors

🐦 The term "conquistador" was used to describe the Spanish explorers who led conquests in the Americas between the fifteenth and nineteenth centuries.

🐦 Why the Americas? The Spanish were motivated by newfound wealth (gold, silver, and spices), power, prestige, expansion of Roman Catholicism, and the development of a Spanish Empire.

🐦 A few years after Cortez conquered the Aztec Empire, Francisco Pizarro (circa 1471–1541) discovered another wealthy empire in Peru known as the Inca Empire. Pizarro managed to capture the king, Atahualpa, and hold him for ransom. Even though the Incans paid his demands, Pizarro had the king executed by strangulation.

🐦 Hernando Cortes (1485–1547) managed to take out the Aztec Empire of five million people with 600 men, 20 horses, and ten small cannons.

🐦 On his deathbed, Mansio Serra de Leguizamon (1512–1589), one of the conquerors of Peru, expressed deep regret for the destruction of the Inca Empire. His last dying words were, "I have to say this now for my conscience: for I am the last to die of the conquistadors."

🐦 The conquistadors' attire was simple: they wore a long-sleeved shirt called a *camisa*, which was accompanied by balloon or pumpkin pants. The look was completed with a *Jacquet de Mala*, a long jacket made of chainmail.

C

❧ Hernando Cortez and his soldiers walked more than 200 miles (320 km) to get to Tenochtitlán, the capital of the Aztec Empire and the so-called "city of gold."

❧ The mortal wound that led to the death of explorer Juan Ponce de León y Figueroa (1474–1521) was inflicted by an arrow poisoned with sap from a manchineel tree.

❧ In Punta Gorda, Florida, there is a memorial plaque which reads, "First White Man Dies in America." The years 1460–1522 are written at the top of the marker, but no name is given.

❧ The Spanish invaders forbid the planting of amaranth because of its use in indigenous religious customs.

❧ The Spanish brought marijuana to America in 1545.

Cook, James

🐦 A life at sea. James Cook (1728–1779) was born the son of a farm worker in Yorkshire and worked on coal ships, known as colliers, before joining the Royal Navy at the age of 26.

🐦 By sailing around the world farther south than anyone had done before, he disproved the long-established theory that there was a southern continent.

🐦 He was the first to chart Australia's east coast and sail around New Zealand.

🐦 In three years, he lost only one crew member.

🐦 The Hawaiian Islands was Cook's first discovery, which he originally named the Sandwich Islands.

🐦 Cook prescribed carrot marmalade and sauerkraut to his crew as a cure for scurvy.

🐦 On February 14, 1779, Cook was killed on Sandwich Island in a riot by the indigenous population. The cause? An argument over a stolen boat.

C

Crimean War

🐦 The Crimean War (1853–56), also known in Russia as the Eastern War, was fought between the Russian Empire and the allied forces of France, England, Sardinia, and Turkey.

🐦 French and British soldiers were dying from disease in filthy, rat-infested hospitals in Turkey. Consequently, Sidney Herbert, Britain's war minister, enlisted the help of Florence Nightingale. By organizing proper military nursing services, she reduced the death toll significantly.

🐦 *The Charge of the Light Brigade* by Lord Alfred Tennyson is a famous poem inspired by the Crimean War and is about courage and the tragedy of war.

🐦 The Crimean War began originally as a religious feud.

🐦 The Crimean War Memorial in London, England, was designed by John Bell and unveiled in 1861. It features statues of three guards standing beneath an allegorical female figure called Honour.

Cuban Missile Crisis

❖ The Cuban Missile Crisis was a major cold war confrontation between the United States and the Soviet Union in 1962. It was the first and only nuclear confrontation between the two countries.

❖ Colonel Oleg Penkovsky (1919–1963)—a CIA spy in the Russian military, who was also known as "Agent Hero"—had informed the United Kingdom and the United States that the Soviet Union was placing missiles on Cuba, which led to the crisis. Penkovsky was arrested by the KGB, found guilty of treason, and executed by a shot in the back of the neck.

❖ *Cuban Missile Crisis: the Aftermath* is a computer game inspired by the true-life event. In the game, the player chooses to take command of one of the four major factions left in a post-World War III world: the Anglo American Alliance; the Soviet Union; the Franco-German Alliance; or China.

C

❖ In Russian history texts, the Cuban Missile Crisis is known as the "Caribbean crisis" while in Cuba, it's called the "Crisis of October."

❖ Hair-raising tales … *Thirteen Days*—starring Kevin Costner—was a movie about the handling of the crisis by President John F. Kennedy, Attorney General Robert Kennedy, and others. In 2001, the movie was nominated for Best Period Hair Styling at the 2001 Hollywood Makeup Artist and Hair Stylist Guild Award.

Curie, Marie

🍂 Marie Curie (1867–1934) was born as Maria Sklodowska and made her mark in history as a renowned and pioneering physicist and chemist.

🍂 She was awarded half of the Nobel prize for physics in 1903, for her and her husband's research into spontaneous radiation. The other half of the prize was awarded to Becquerel, who discovered this science. As a major contributor to the world of science, this was just one of two Nobel Prizes which she earned during her lifetime.

🍂 The Marie Curie Cancer Care Charity based in the UK employs more than 2,700 nurses, doctors and other healthcare professionals, and provides care to approximately 29,000 terminally ill patients each year.

🍂 Four years after her husband Pierre died in a road accident, the 43-year-old widow began a love affair with a married scientist who was five years her junior. They would rendezvous in an apartment in Sorbonne, France.

🍂 As the "Mother of Modern Physics", Curie was a woman who was passionate about sciences and its contribution to humanity. She even received a gift of $50,000 in 1929 from President Herbert Hoover, which had been donated by the American Friends of Science.

Czars

❧ Ivan the Terrible (1530–1584) was the first ruler to use the term "czar" in Russia. On one occasion he even threw cats and dogs out of the Kremlin window, and it is believed he suffered from a mental illness that was quite likely bipolar disorder.

❧ The last Czar of Russia, Nicolas II (1868–1918), his wife Alexandra, and Kaiser Wilhelm II of Germany (1859–1941) were all first cousins of King George V (1865–1936) of the United Kingdom.

❧ Czar power … In May 1896, Nicholas II was formally crowned Czar of Russia. A large celebration was held in Khodynka Field outside Moscow, where free food, beer, and souvenirs were offered. In the ensuing stampede, 1,389 were killed and some 1,300 injured.

C

❧ The term "czar" is sometimes used for high-level civil servants, such as the "drug czar," "terrorism czar," and "war czar."

❧ The first ruler other than a Russian to adopt the title czar was Simeon I of Bulgaria (circa 864–927).

❧ The last person to hold the title of czar was Simeon Saxe-Coburg-Gotha (born 1937), the last czar of Bulgaria (1943–46) before being exiled. He made it back to power, however, this time as prime minister of the Republic of Bulgaria from 2001–5.

❧ What do you call a czar in training? A czarevich! This was the title used for the heir apparent to the position of emperor of Russia.

Declaration of Independence

- There were 56 signers of the American Declaration of Independence.

- After the Declaration of Independence had been written and signed, printer John Dunlap published 200 copies to be distributed throughout the colonies. A "Dunlap Broadside," as each copy became known, is extremely rare and valuable, and there are only 26 known to be in existence today.

- Contrary to popular belief, the declaration was signed on August 2, 1776, and not on July 4, 1776.

D

- Jefferson originally included language condemning the British promotion of the slave trade. Funnily enough, he was actually a slave owner himself.

- In the summer of 1776, when the Declaration was signed, the population of the U.S. was an estimated 2.5 million.

Democracy

❧ New Zealand was the first democratic nation to give voting rights in 1893 to both men and women.

❧ India is the world's largest democracy.

❧ Direct democracy, where the whole community meets to make laws, occurred as early as 5 B.C.E. in Athens, Greece.

❧ When Andrew Jackson ran for president in 1828, his opponents tried to label him a "jackass" for his views and his slogan, "Let the people rule." Andrew found some humor in this by having a donkey on his campaign posters.

❧ According to Indian economist and philosopher, Amartya Sen, the winner of the 1998 Nobel Memorial Prize in Economic Science, "no famine has ever taken place in the history of the world in a functioning democracy."

D

Democratic Republic of Timor-Leste

◦❧ Also known as East Timor, this is a small country in Southeast Asia that recently attained its independence. In May 2002, East Timor became the first new sovereign state of the twenty-first century, making it the world's newest country.

◦❧ Even though Tetum and Portuguese are the official languages, Indonesian and English are the working languages of the East Timorese.

◦❧ Despite being a tiny country situated in Southeast Asia, the currency of East Timor is the U.S. dollar.

D

◦❧ East Timor, along with the Philippines, are the only two primarily Roman Catholic countries in Southeast Asia.

◦❧ The 1996 Nobel Peace Prize was shared between two East Timorese—journalist Jose Ramos-Horta and Bishop Carlos Bela—for their work toward achieving peace in East Timor.

Despots

~ Idi Amin Dada (1925–2003) was a former heavyweight-boxing champion before he became the military dictator and self-appointed president of Uganda during the 1970s.

~ Enlightened despotism is a form of rule where the ruler's reason is advocated as the primary source for legitimacy and authority. Notable Enlightened Despots included Frederick the Great, Catherine the Great, and Joseph II.

~ Soviet dictator Joseph Stalin (1878–1953), one of the most ruthless despots of modern times, was born Ioseb Besarionis dze Jughashvili in Georgia. He allegedly changed his name in an attempt to hide his Georgian roots. His adopted name Stalin means "Man of Steel."

~ President Truman once described Stalin as a "little squirt." Standing at 5 foot, 5 inches (1.6 m), Stalin was notoriously sensitive about his height and had several portrait painters executed for failing to capture his godliness.

~ North Korea has a long association with Zimbabwean dictator Robert Mugabe, having trained the Zimbabwe army brigade responsible for the massacre of at least 20,000 people in the 1980s. In 2010 Mugabe thanked fellow despot, Kim Jong Il with an "ark" of animals.

D

Dinosaurs

- Crocodiles and birds are the closest living relatives to the dinosaur.

- Does size really matter? Most dinosaurs were up to 89 feet (27 m) tall, but some were as small as chickens.

- Drumheller Museum in Alberta, Canada, boasts the largest collection of complete dinosaur skeletons. Seventy million years ago, parts of the Great White North were actually tropical.

- Purple reign! Barney, the beloved playtime dinosaur, was originally intended to be a bear. It was only after the creator, Sheryl Leach took her son to a dinosaur exhibit that the character became a dinosaur.

D

- Ferdinand Vandiveer Hayden made the first discovery of dinosaur remains in 1854 along the upper Missouri River.

- Today, paleontologists have identified and named 700 different species of dinosaurs. One of the most intelligent dinosaurs was Troodon, a 6-foot (2-m) long hunting dinosaur with the brain size of a mammal.

Dresden Bombing

❧ Dresden, Germany, was a crucial commercial and transportation center in Germany at the time of the bombings during World War II, in 1945.

❧ The policy of bombing Dresden from the air was agreed upon at the Yalta conference between the United States, the United Kingdom, and the Soviet Union in the same year. The bombs were targeted at major oil plants, tanks, factories, and aircraft factories of the Nazi empire. Unfortunately these were all located around a major civilian population.

❧ Three thousand three hundred tons of bombs were dropped on the city over three waves of attacks. Many of these incendiary bombs created so much fire that the more the city burned, the more oxygen was sucked in. Temperatures were thought to have peaked at 1,800° F (980°C).

❧ The incendiary bombs were made of magnesium concentrate.

❧ Although there were no fewer than 18 railroad stations in the city, only one was bombed and it was back in operation three days later.

❧ During the bombing, 135,000 people died, more than the death toll of Hiroshima and Nagasaki combined.

D

Dutch History

- The Dutch East India Company monopolized the spice trade of the seventeenth century and established trading ports all over Asia. They were the first company to issue public stock.

- Dutch people are some of the tallest in the world with average height of 6 feet (184 cm) for men and 5 feet 6 inches (170 cm) for women.

- Up until the sixteenth century, carrots in the Netherlands had been white, yellow, black, purple, or red. Orange carrots were bred in honor of the House of Orange, who led the Dutch Revolt against Spain (1568–1609) and eventually became the Dutch Royal family.

D
- Gin was invented in the Netherlands and first sold as a medicine in the late sixteenth century. It was to be another 250 years before the Brits started enjoying gin and tonics.

- The Dutch originally built windmills for corn milling, saw milling, and land drainage.

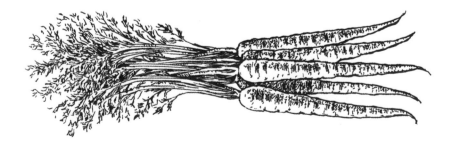

Earhart, Amelia

❧ In 1932, Amelia Earhart was the first woman to ever fly solo across the Atlantic Ocean and also the first female to receive the Airforce Distinguished Flying Cross.

❧ Hollywood actress and Oscar winner Hilary Swank starred as the flying heroine in the biopic, *Amelia*.

❧ Her death was enshrouded in mystery. She disappeared while she was en route from Lae, New Guinea to Howland Island. The search for Amelia was the most expensive and intensive air and sea search at that time, costing the U.S. government $4 million.

❧ Earhart was nicknamed "Lady Lindy" because of her slender frame and facial resemblance to Charles Lindbergh.

❧ Amelia once said, "The woman who can create her own job is the woman who will win fame and fortune."

E

Egyptian Cult of the Dead

- The Ancient Egyptians had a fear of death and mummification provided a sense of immortality.

- Kebechet, a goddess of the underworld, was depicted as a serpent.

- The average Egyptian was generally a poor peasant and though it is likely the peasants believed in an afterlife, they did not have the means to build themselves lavish tombs. Therefore, the ancient cult of the dead was likely based on the doctrines of the upper class.

E

- A dead body would be washed with wine and spices before it was mummified.

- Dear John ... Between the late Old Kingdom to the late New Kingdom, letters were written to the dead. A relative inscribed a message on a bowl and placed it in the tomb of the deceased in the belief that by writing a letter to the dead, the spirit of the deceased could help to protect them from ill fortune.

- Some might say *The Book of the Dead* was a tome for a tomb. This comprehensive guide served to provide readers with the funerary rites and mummification procedure to ensure the deceased made a safe journey to their final resting place. Earliest known versions date from the sixteenth century B.C.E.

Eisenhower, Dwight

❧ The 34th U.S. President, Eisenhower (1890–1969) had a humble upbringing and climbed the ranks of the army. He began World War II as Lt. Colonel and by December 1944 he reached the five-star rank of General of the Army.

❧ Eisenhower's initiative to send federal troops into Little Rock, Arkansas, to ensure that local schools were desegregated was an important step in the Civil Rights movement.

❧ He was also the first president licensed to fly a plane.

❧ Eisenhower endorsed the U.S. Interstate Highway Act, in 1956. The 11,000-mile (66,000-km) highway system was the largest public works program in U.S. history at the time.

E

❧ He was the first president to appear on color television and the first president of all 50 states.

❧ Take this fact at face value: Eishenhower's portrait was on the silver dollar from 1971 to 1978.

Eleanor of Aquitaine

- Beautiful and charismatic, Eleanor (1122–1204) inherited the Duchy of Aquitaine when she was 15 years old.

- Eleanor of Aquitaine was renowned for her powerful personality. She led her sons to rebel (unsuccessfully) against their father, King Henry II (1133–1189). Consequently, he put her under house arrest for 15 years.

- Eleanor had her marriage to her first husband Louis VII of France annulled on the grounds of consanguinity or, in layman's terms, being too closely related by blood. Eleanor claimed that Louis VII's infrequent visits to her bed led to the ruin of their marriage.

E
- Eleanor regained possession of Aquitaine and Poitou. With wealth and beauty on her side, she attracted suitors well before the annulment of her first marriage to Louis VII. One notable man, Henry of Anjou (a domain bordering Poitou), expressed much interest in Eleanor who was rumored to have had an affair with his father, Geoffrey of Anjou. Regardless of this, 30-year-old Eleanor and 18-year-old Henry felt passionately for each other.

Emancipation
of Women

❧ Throughout the 1800s, court cases involving the sale of wives were more common than we'd expect. Some husbands believed that if a wife was taken to market with a halter or a rope around her neck, the sale was legal. The magistrates and newspaper reporters expressed disgust at the sheer ignorance of such behavior.

❧ The word "woman" is said to have come from the Middle English term *wyfman*, or wife (*wyf*) of man.

❧ American feminist Gloria Steinem once said of the fairer sex, "A liberated woman is one who has sex before marriage and a job after."

❧ Giving with one hand while taking away with the other! The Utah Territory welcomed the enfranchisement of women in 1870, but then Congress withheld the right in 1887. It was not until Utah became a state in 1896 that women regained their right to vote.

❧ A suffrage proposal was put before the Dakota Territory legislature in 1872 and lost—but only by one vote.

❧ In 1848, the first U.S. women's rights convention was held in Seneca Falls, New York. After two days of discussion and debate, 68 women and 32 men signed a Declaration of Sentiments, which outlined grievances and set the agenda for the women's rights movement.

E

Empress Wu Zetian

- Confucious once stated that having a woman rule would be as unnatural as having a "hen crow like a rooster at daybreak." Empress Wu Zetian (625–705), the only female in Chinese history to rule as emperor, certainly proved him wrong.

- Born into a rich and noble family, Zetian was taught to play music, write, and read the Chinese classics.

- At the age of 13, she was already known for her sharp wit, intelligence, and beauty. She was the favored of Emperor Tai Tsung, but was far more interested in his son, Kao Tsung.

- Wu began a campaign to promote girl power. She commissioned scholars to write biographies of famous women, and raised the position of her mother's clan by giving her relatives high political posts.

- During her near 50 years of reign, Empress Wu chose Buddhism over Daoism as the favored state religion. Chinese Buddhism achieved its highest development in this time.

- Despite having formed a powerful centralized regime, and creating a prosperous national economy and stable social order, she was far from perfect. She killed her sons and her baby daughter to protect and achieve her political ambitions.

England

❧ The word Anglican comes from the term "Angles," which is used to describe the original settlers of England in the tenth century.

❧ Tennis, soccer, and cricket were first played in England.

❧ What did Henry VI and King Edward IV share in common? They were the only two British monarchs to have reigned more than once: Henry VI ruled between 1422–1461 and 1470–1471 and Edward IV from 1461–1470 and 1471–1483.

❧ *History of Troy* was the first book to be printed in English in 1474. William Caxton (circa 1422–1492), an English merchant and author, not only wrote the book about the ancient Greek city, he also introduced the printing press to England. How resourceful!

❧ All men may be created equal, but not all created equal. Robert Recorde (1510–1558), a London doctor and mathematic genius of Welsh origin, developed the equal sign (=) in mathematics.

❧ Between the eighteenth and early nineteenth centuries, English laws protected the interest and property of the rich and punishment for the pettiest of crimes was execution. Known as The Bloody Code, it was the most brutal punishment and penal system in the Western world at the time. You could be hanged for stealing goods worth 5 shillings (40 cents), destroying a turnpike, or cutting down a young tree.

E

❧ From 1066 to 1362, French was the official language of England.

❧ That's tasty, baby! The drought of 682 C.E. was so bad that the Saxons in the south of England ate their way through all their food and livestock and eventually ate their children!

❧ In 1563 Elizabeth I passed a law stating that no person could eat meat on Wednesdays, Fridays, or Sundays. This was to encourage people to become fishermen, and by becoming fishermen, they had to learn how to sail, and thus became excellent candidates for the navy if a war started.

❧ Charles II (1630–1685) escaped the anti-Royalists when he lost the battle of Worcester (1651) by hiding up an oak tree. This is why the Oak Apple became his symbol when he was crowned king.

❧ Lord Horatio Nelson (1758–1805) who defeated the French at the Battle of Trafalgar suffered from sea sickness.

English Language

 The English language started not with the English, but with the arrival of three Germanic tribes—the Angles, the Saxons, and the Jutes—who invaded Britain during the fifth century. Prior to the invasion, the inhabitants spoke a Celtic language.

 The English colonization of North America naturally led to a distinct variation of the language. Some words the British now consider to be "Americanisms" are trash (rubbish), fall (autumn), and loan used as a verb (lend). These words are originally British, but fell out of fashion in the mother country while they were preserved in the colonies.

 English continuously integrates foreign words, especially Latin and Greek, into the language. As a result, English has the largest vocabulary of any language in the world.

E

 Samuel Johnson (1709–1784) was paid 1,500 guineas to compile the *Dictionary of the English Language*, which was published in 1755. It took nine years to complete and contained the definition of more than 40,000 words.

 "Almost" is the longest word in the English language with all the letters in alphabetical order.

 Our letter "N" is most likely derived from the Egyptian hieroglyph depicting a viper.

- Shakespeare (1564–1616) is credited with adding 1,700 words to the English language. The additions we can thank him for are critic, majestic, exposure, and lonely.

- "Y'all" was first used in the Southern United States in the early 1900s.

- P.M. comes from Latin, "post meridian," meaning "after noon."

- The uncle of Peter Mark Roget, publisher of *Roget's Thesaurus*, killed himself while in the presence of his nephew.

- The first autobiography in English was written by an illiterate mother of 14 children named Margery Kempe (1373–1438). She dictated her story.

- In the mid-1400s a Welsh Bishop named Reginald Pecock attempted to get rid of certain Latin words in hopes of purifying the English language. Among his suggestions was the substitution of "impenetrable" with "ungothroughsome."

Environmental Movement

🕊️ The Environmental Movement is a term used to describe social, scientific, and political organizations that address environmental issues.

🕊️ Chico Mendez (1944–1988) was a Brazilian environmental activist who fought to stop logging in the Amazon rainforest for cattle ranching and was murdered for his cause.

🕊️ According to Andrew Rowell—investigative journalist and author of *Green Backlash*—the largest and most influential environmental organizations in the United States are the "Group of Ten": Defenders of Wildlife, Environmental Defense Fund, National Audubon Society, National Wildlife Federation, Natural Resources Defense Council, Friends of the Earth, Izaak Walton League, Sierra Club, The Wilderness Society, and the World Wide Fund for Nature.

🕊️ Al Gore held the first congressional hearings on climate change and was also known as one of the Atari Democrats, later called the "Democrats' Greens," who were politicians who supported and rallied issues like clean air, clean water, and global warming.

🕊️ Al Gore appeared as himself as his own head jar in an episode of Matt Groening's animated sitcom *Futurama*.

🕊️ King Edward I made the first air pollution law in 1273, in hopes of cutting down on the smog in London.

E

❧ Emulation of the Queen of France, Marie Antoinette's (1755–1793) hairstyles led to the Beehives and Bouffants of the 1950s and '60s and eventually to aerosol hairspray, to keep them in place. The chloro-fluorocarbons they released contributed to damage to the ozone layer.

❧ In 1888, poet William Wordsworth referred to the Industrial Revolution as an "outrage done to nature" (*The Excursion, Book Eighth*).

❧ In 2006, the United Nations Food and Agriculture Organization found that cow flatulence was a greater source of greenhouse gas emissions than car exhaust fumes.

❧ Fresh Kills Landfill in Staten Island, NY, is visible from outer space.

❧ The disposable bottle and can came into being in the 1930s. In 1934, the national Recovery Administration established a deposit ranging from two to five cents.

Etruscans

❧ The Etruscans who were known as Tyrrhenians by the Greeks, lived in the area of Italy now known as Tuscany. Their civilization greatly influenced Roman religion, art, architecture, and education.

❧ There were only 20 distinct characters in their alphabet.

❧ No existing written documents were written in complete sentences.

❧ The Etruscans introduced tile roofs to Italy.

❧ A fact worthy of a smile ... Etruscans had developed some form of dentistry as proven by the many dental bridges and partial gold dentures found in the tombs. They would've dated about 500 B.C.E.

E

❧ Very little is known about this civilization. The Emperor Claudius (10 B.C.E.–54 C.E.) who married an Etruscan princess named Urgulanilla, is said to have written an elaborate, 20-book history on the Estrucans. Sadly, the books got lost.

❧ The famous Roman toga was a variation on an Etruscan cloak.

❧ Herbs such as bay leaf and rosemary were used freely in Etruscan cooking. Wine was added to many recipes for extra flavor.

❧ Etruscans danced and played music during funerals, and also played games involving throwing disks and climbing poles.

Explorers

✦ The fact that the Earth is round was generally accepted long before Christopher Columbus (1451–1506) discovered the Americas. Egyptian-Greek scientist Erastosthenes (276–195 B.C.E.) was hailed for his calculations of the diameter of the Earth, working for the cities of Alexandria and Aswan, and had already measured the circumference. Around 350 B.C.E., the Greek philosopher and thinker Aristotle proved it after an observation that the Earth casts a spherical shadow on the Moon during an eclipse.

✦ While confined to a Genoese prison for two years, the Italian explorer Marco Polo (circa 1254–1324) dictated his experiences of the Far East to a fellow prisoner named Rustichello da Pisa. The account was carefully written out and the book *The Travels of Marco Polo* has been translated into numerous languages.

✦ Estavanico, a Moroccan slave, accompanied Cabeza de Vaca on his explorations of southwestern USA in the 1500s and was the first black man to set foot on North American soil.

✦ The mineral, armalcolite, discovered during the first Moon landing and later found at various locations on the Earth, was named after the three Apollo 11 astronauts, Neil Armstrong, Buzz Aldrin, and Michael Collins.

✦ In 1943, French oceanographer and naval officer Jacques Cousteau (1910–1997) co-invented (with Émil Gagnan) the first self-contained underwater breathing apparatus. They called it the aqua-lung.

Falkland Islands

🐦 In 1592, the English navigator John Davis made the first confirmed sighting of the Islands.

🐦 The Falkland Islands were thought to be unoccupied when Europeans first visited them, but the recent discoveries of arrowheads in the southern half of East Falkland and the remains of a wooden canoe suggest that people—most likely the Yaghan people of Tierra del Fuego—had visited there first.

🐦 When English naturalist Charles Darwin (1809–1882) visited the island during the early 1830s, he collected flora, fauna, and fossils important to the conception of his book *On the Origin of Species* (1859) and also observed features known as "stone runs" and the numerous shipwrecks around the Islands.

🐦 The size of the island is 7,564 square miles (12,200 km²), just slightly smaller than the state of Connecticut.

🐦 The Falkland Islands enjoy almost crime-free status with little civil disobedience … except for that time in 2008 when $1.5 million dollars worth of cocaine disappeared from a double-locked cell at a police station.

F

Fascism

❧ Fascism is an extreme authoritarian and nationalistic right-wing system of government and social organization.

❧ Mussolini (1883–1945), the founder of fascism and leader of Italy from 1922–1943, was allies with Nazi Germany and Japan in World War II. In 2009, his granddaughter Alessandra claimed that his blood and parts of his brain had been stolen from a hospital in Milan to sell on the Internet.

❧ In October 1967, Jim Garrison, the District Attorney best known for his investigations into the assassination of JFK, once said, "I'm afraid, based on my own experience, that fascism will come to America in the name of national security."

❧ The Iron Guard was a fascist movement and political party based in Romania from 1927–1941. It was strongly anti-Semitic and they considered ideas such as freemasonry, Freudianism, atheism, Marxism, bolshevism, the civil war in Spain, and social democracy to undermine society.

❧ Dennis Lawrence, once described by *Life* magazine as "America's number one intellectual fascist," led the American fascist movement of the 1930s. He was a fan of Hitler, a self-avowed anti-Semite, and a light-skinned African-American, born in the segregated South.

Fashion

🐦 A rally of support. The bra was patented in 1914 and created by a New York socialist named Mary Phelps who was tired of having her camisole show when she wore a lacy blouse. The first version was made with two handkerchiefs.

🐦 Men were the first to wear jewelry as a status symbol and during battle as good luck amulets.

🐦 In the 1930s, women in Bermuda were forbidden to show their thighs in public. However, locals and visitors wanted to wear shorts to stay cool in the Caribbean heat, so shorts were lengthened to the knees.

🐦 In 1571, during the rule of Queen Elizabeth I, a law was created that called for anyone over the age of seven to wear a hat on Sundays. Though the law no longer exists in England, people still wear hats to attend prominent events, such as horse races, garden parties, and weddings, and this can be accredited to Elizabeth I.

F

❧ Coco Chanel (1883–1971), French fashion guru once said, "Fashion fades. Only style remains."

❧ Pioneering women reformers began wearing long pantaloons under shorter skirts. The name of American Amelia Bloomer, an advocate for the style, was adopted to refer to the ballooned-out pants (bloomers) she wore. Women wearing bloomers were so mocked that they ultimately gave the fashion up. Of the whole episode, American Elizabeth Caty Stanton's father wrote that, "no woman of good sense and delicacy" would "make a guy of herself."

❧ Henry II, King of Germany and Holy Roman Emperor (973–1024) is credited with the invention of the pocket. His were made of silk.

❧ The gold miners in the 1849 California Gold Rush were the first to wear blue jeans.

❧ A 1370 law in Strasbourg determined that, "no woman should support her bust, whether by arranging her chemise or by lacing her dress" so as to unnaturally augment her breast size. As if it were any of the lawmakers' business!

❧ The Beatles wore "Nehru jackets" and contributed to the giant fad they became. The man for whom the jacket had been a tradition— Jawaharial Nehru, prime minister of India from 1947–1964—was featured in *Vogue* magazine wearing one and helped move the trend along.

Feminism

- Betty Friedan's book *The Feminine Mystique* (1963) attacked the idea that women can only be wives and mothers.

- Samuel Johnson (1709–1784) may have been a much-lauded author, but not a feminist supporter. He once said, "Nature has given women so much power that the law has very wisely given them little."

- "If women are supposed to be less rational and more emotional at the beginning of our menstrual cycle when the female hormone is at its lowest level, then why isn't it logical to say that, in those few days, women behave the most like the way men behave all month long?" Gloria Steinem had a very good point.

- The earliest recorded female physician was Merit Ptah, a doctor in Ancient Egypt who lived around 2700 B.C.E. Many historians believe she is the first woman recorded by name in the history of all of the sciences.

- In 1890, Wyoming became the first state with women's suffrage.

- The first elected female leader to rule a country was Sirimavo Bandaranaike of Sri Lanka. She was elected as prime minister in 1960 and later re-elected in 1970.

F

Feudalism

- Feudalism is a term used to describe the exchange of land for military service. King William the Conqueror employed this system following the defeat of Hastings in 1066 and rewarded his soldiers for their help in conquering England.

- In a feudal agreement, one who receives the land is known as a vassal.

- Vassals received more than land from the lords. They were given estates that included houses, tools, barns, animals, and peasants, who were more commonly known as serfs. The serfs were essentially slaves who were bound to the land, even when it was sold.

F

- In Feudal Japan between 1185 and 1603, society was divided into two classes—nobility and peasants. The noble class comprised of 12 percent of the population.

- In 2008, 450 years of feudalism came to an end on the Island of Sark. Located 80 miles (130 km) off the south coast of England, it had been governed by a combination of landowners and elected people since the seventeenth century.

First Ladies

🍂 Lucy Ware Webb Hayes, wife of U.S. President Rutherford B. Hayes, not only abstained from drinking alcohol, but banned its consumption in the White House. For this reason, she was nicknamed Lemonade Lucy.

🍂 Grace Coolidge once taught at a school for the deaf.

🍂 Dolley Madison came from a modest Quaker background, but loved to dress up and always had a box of snuff at her side.

🍂 Sculpture is one of Hilary Clinton's favorite art forms. Her first date with Bill Clinton was in the sculpture garden at Yale University.

🍂 "The one thing I do not want to be called is first lady. It sounds like a saddle horse." Jackie Kennedy Onassis.

F

Fortaleza, La

- La Fortaleza is the official current residence of the Governor of Puerto Rico. Completed in 1540, it's the oldest governor's mansion of the Western Hemisphere as well as the island's first fortress.

- The mansion has a broken, old mahogany clock that stands in a corridor. Ricardo De Ortega, the last Spanish governor, paused in front of this clock and struck its face with his sword before relinquishing the building. The time the clock stopped at represents the last moment the Spanish ruled in Puerto Rico.

- UNESCO proclaimed La Fortaleza as a World Heritage Site in 1983.

- On May 26, 2004, a man armed with a knife entered the mansion's mailroom and took a receptionist hostage. A near three-hour standoff ended after the governor entered the building and read the hostage taker's letter demanding a house and a job.

- Admission to the mansion is $3 and one must be dressed respectfully—nothing above the knee and no sleeveless shirts.

Frank, Anne

🐦 After the Nazi's rise to power, Anne's father got scared and like many Jews at the time, moved the family to the Netherlands where he found work. Anne stayed back with her granny during the move and joined the family on her sister Margot's eighth birthday.

🐦 Anne's father set up a company called Opekta in Amsterdam, which sold jam-making supplies.

🐦 Eventually Amsterdam was no longer a safe place for Jews to live openly so the family went into hiding. Anne had to wear all her clothes because carrying suitcases would have aroused suspicion that the family was trying to escape. She wore two undershirts, three pairs of pants, a skirt, a dress, a jacket, a raincoat, two pairs of stockings, heavy shoes, a cap, and a scarf.

🐦 Anne loved movie stars, reading Greek myths, riding her bicycle, and making trips to the local ice-cream parlor.

🐦 While the family were in hiding Anne kept a diary. It was first published in Dutch in 1947. Since then, it has been translated into 60 languages and sold more than 25 million copies worldwide.

🐦 *The Diary of Anne Frank* ... the musical? A Spanish theater transformed her story into a musical production in 2008.

F

Franklin, Benjamin

❧ Benjamin Franklin (1705–1790) was not only one of the Founding Fathers of the United States, he was also an author, printer, satirist, scientist, and inventor.

❧ Some of Franklin's inventions included the glass harmonica (a musical instrument) and bifocals.

❧ Poultry in motion? Not quite. In 1789, Franklin proposed that the turkey replace the bald-headed eagle as the national symbol of the United States. Luckily no one seems to have been paying much attention.

❧ It's all about the Benjamins, baby … Franklin's portrait has been on the $100 bill since 1928.

❧ The future Founding Father became a vegetarian at age 16 for health reasons and to save money in order to buy more books.

❧ Benjamin Franklin is part of the International Swimming Hall of Fame. Among his many inventions are swimming fins to wear on your hands.

❧ Some of Franklin's *noms de plume* were: Silence Dogood, Polly Baker, and Richard Saunders.

F

Frederick the Great

🍂 Frederick the Great (1712–1786) was the king of Prussia. He built his reputation by commanding the War of the Austrian Succession (1740–48), defeating all European powers that were involved, and gaining new territory with limited resources.

🍂 In 1774 he ordered his subjects to grow potatoes to provide food and to lower the price of bread. People were reluctant and in Kolberg, they complained, "The things have neither smell nor taste. Not even the dogs will eat them. So what use are they to us?"

🍂 The statue in Berlin, Germany, of Frederick the Great astride his favorite horse is said to have taken nearly 70 years, 40 artists, and 100 designs to complete.

🍂 He is quoted as saying, "If my soldiers were to begin to think, not one would remain in the ranks."

🍂 As an 18-year-old, the future king of Prussia saw his lover, Lieutenant Hans Hermann von Katte beheaded by order of his father.

🍂 Women were not permitted in the king's lavish Potsdam Palace, built after the Seven Years' War (1756–1763).

🍂 Frederick once attempted a prohibition on coffee because he believed it compromised the effectiveness of soldiers. He even created a special force unit in Germany called *Kaffee Schnufflers* (coffee sniffers) to hunt out soldiers who smelled like they might have been indulging in it.

F

French Colonialism

- At its peak in the early part of the twentieth century, the French Empire possessed nearly 10 percent of the world's land area.

- *Pardonnez-vous?* French ranks fourth as the most-spoken language in the United States behind English, Spanish, and Chinese.

- In 1498, France claimed the area of Canada and Maine and called it Acadia.

- The French settled along the St. Lawrence and Mississippi rivers and under the law were allowed to trade furs, lumber, and fish, but only with France or other French colonies.

- In 1801 in Haiti, ex-slave Toussaint L'Ouverture led nearly one-half million Haitian slaves against Haiti's French colonialists. Their victory was the first successful slave revolt and helped to establish Haiti as the first black republic.

F

French Revolution

~❧ The French Revolution (1789–1799) violently transformed France from an absolute monarchy with strict social classes into a nation with a more relaxed social structure.

~❧ King Louis XVI's wife, Marie Antoinette (1755–1793), commonly dressed and bathed in front of 40 people!

~❧ Bread cost more than one week's salary before the revolution began.

~❧ Marie Antoinette was a style icon in her day. It's been reported that while at the opera, eight women were injured just to get a glimpse of what she was wearing.

~❧ During the so-called Reign of Terror (1793–94), everyone was afraid that that day would be their last. Anyone reported as behaving suspiciously or as being a traitor to the new government would be taken captive and later executed at the guillotine. More than 15,000 people were beheaded.

F

Gandhi, Indira

- Indira Gandhi (1917–1984) was the prime minister of the Republic of India for three consecutive terms from 1966 to 1977. To date, she is the world's all-time longest-serving female Prime Minister.

- When she was four years old, her father and grandfather were first jailed for their political activities.

- She was not in fact Mahatma Ghandi's daughter, but the daughter of a friend of Ghandi's called Jawaharlal Nehru. Her surname was owed to her marriage to Feroze Gandhi, an Indian politician and journalist.

- Delhi's international airport was named in her honor.

G

- On October 31, 1984, Gandhi was assassinated by her two bodyguards, Satwant Singh and Beant Singh. Her death sparked a round of sectarian violence.

- Her son Rajiv, was sworn in as her successor within hours of her death. He was assassinated by a suicide bomber on May 21, 1991.

Gang of Four

🍂 The Gang of Four was a powerful and influential band of radical political elite who implemented the harsh policies of the Chinese Communist Party (CCP) during the Cultural Revolution (1966–1976) led by Mao Zedong (1893–1976). The group included Wang Hongwen, Zhang Chunqiao, Yao Wenyuan, and Jiang Qing, Mao's third wife.

🍂 Jiang Qing (1914–1991), the daughter of a carpenter, worked as a stage and movie actress in Shanghai before she joined the CCP.

🍂 When put on a highly publicized trial for anti-party activities, torture, and framing or persecuting 700,000 people, Zhang refused to speak or to look at any of the evidence presented at his trial. He was sentenced to death but this was commuted to life imprisonment.

G

🍂 Yao Wenyuan, the last surviving member of the Gang of Four, died n January 2004 at the age of 74.

🍂 Gang of Four was also the name of a radical punk band from the late seventies, who used unconventional funk and reggae rhythms in their music.

Gold Rush

~◆ Lumberman James Marshall discovered the first gold nuggets in California on January 24, 1848, while building a saw mill on the American River. The discovery inspired nearly every ambitious young man and women to move there in search of gold.

~◆ People traveled from as far away as China, Turkey, Germany, and France to join the rush. Many left home in 1849, and so were nicknamed the "forty-niners."

~◆ Women mined another kind of gold during the Rush. Domestic skills were in considerable demand and women could earn a pretty penny by preparing simple meals in Dutch ovens.

G

~◆ The hygienic conditions were deplorable. In summer, prospectors sweated profusely in 90°F (32°C) heat but there was nowhere to take a shower or baths. In addition, they often had little choice but to drink rancid water, which caused diarrhea.

~◆ Because of poor planning, many western-bound forty-niners were unprepared for the hot, dry deserts of Nevada. A few sharp businessmen in California knew this and took advantage of the situation. They traveled eastward with barrels of water. Extremely thirsty, many forty-niners paid $1, $5, even $100 for a glass of water.

Grant, Ulysses

❧ As eighteenth President of the U.S., Ulysses S. Grant is arguably one of the worst in America's history. His term (1869–1877) was marked by five major scandals.

❧ One of the scandals involved the Crédit Mobilier in 1872. In order to cover up stealing money from the Union Pacific Railroad, the major stockholders of the railroad company created Crédit Mobilier of America to divert its construction profits. The perpetrators also gave or sold stock cheaply to influential members of Congress.

❧ President Grant's real name was Hiram Ulysses Grant, but he changed it. Maybe the monogram H.U.G. wasn't big and manly enough.

❧ After his presidency, Grant became a partner in a financial firm in the 1880s, which went bankrupt.

❧ About that time he learned that he had cancer of the throat. He started writing his recollections to pay off his debts and provide for his family, racing against death to produce a memoir that ultimately earned nearly $450,000. Soon after completing the last page, in 1885, he died.

G

Great Depression, The

 The Great Depression was the longest and most widespread global economic depression of the twentieth century. It lasted from about 1929 until the late 1930s—and in some cases into the 1940s. The initial Wall Street crash that caused the Great Depression was so bad that a wave of suicides hit New York's financial district. Clerks of one hotel even started asking new guests if they needed a room for sleeping or jumping.

 In the U.S., people who lost their homes often lived in "Hoovervilles," or shanty towns, named after President Herbert Hoover (1874–1964), who allegedly let the nation slide into depression. There was also "Hoover Stew," which was the food dished out in soup kitchens, "Hoover Blankets," which were newspapers that served as bedding, "Hoover Hogs," which was the term for jack rabbits used as food. Meanwhile "Hoover Wagons" were broken cars that were pulled by mules.

 Things got so bad that even the Chicago gangster Al Capone (1899–1947) opened a soup kitchen during the Great Depression.

 In order not to be seen begging for change many people took up apple selling and in New York City alone there were as many as 6,000 apple sellers.

 While the Great Depression affected most of the U.S. it is estimated that up to 40 percent of the population never had to endure any real hardship at all.

Great Famine, Ireland

- Between 1846 and 1850, the population of Ireland dropped by two million, or 25 percent. One million died of starvation after the potato crop failed, or the diseases associated with the potato famine, and one million emigrated to North America or parts of Britain.

- People who could not afford to buy other food were forced to eat rotten potatoes and contracted diseases such as typhoid.

- Private relief was offered. During 1846–47, the Quakers gave approximately £200,000 for relief in Ireland. They donated food such as American flour, rice, biscuits, and Indian meal, as well as clothing and bedding.

- In spite of the failed potato crop and famine across the country, Ireland was still producing and exporting enough grains to have fed the entire population.

- The name of the fungus that led to the potato blight was *Phytophthora Infestans*. It was caused by an excessive rainfall.

- The journey to the United States at the time of the potato blight cost the equivalent of $10.

- Four decades after the famine, scientists found out how to get rid of the fungus.

G

Great Fire
of London, The

🐚 The Great Fire of London took place in 1666. It was ignited by the unextinguished ashes of a fire at a bakery in Pudding Lane that quickly spread. The resulting inferno lasted for five days.

🐚 Half of London's population was rendered homeless.

🐚 St. Paul's Cathedral was one of 89 churches destroyed.

🐚 After the fire, to prevent a recurrence, houses were built of brick (and not wood) and had flat frontages.

G

🐚 Look at the bright side. The Great Fire of London may have destroyed much of the center of London, but it also killed off most of the rats and fleas carrying the plague known as the Black Death.

Great Migrations

🐦 The Great Migration is the name given to the social phenomenon that started during the early twentieth century when millions of African-Americans traveled across America in pursuit of better economic opportunity.

🐦 Prior to the first Great Migration, approximately 90 percent of African-Americans resided in the South in former slave-holding states, and three out of four lived and worked on farms.

🐦 One of the possible causes for the first Great Migration was the tiny boll weevil. In the late 1910s it had infested and destroyed many of the cotton fields in the southern U.S., putting many people out of work.

G

🐦 During the 1920s, Harlem became the top destination for African-Americans and by 1920, 200,000 were living in Upper Manhattan. Only 15 years earlier the area had been almost totally inhabited by white people.

🐦 During the first Great Migration "blockbusting" was a practice started by U.S. realtors and building developers. In order to get white homeowners to sell their properties at a loss, they would lie to the locals that African-Americans and other ethnic minorities were moving into their neighborhoods, sometimes even paying black people to walk down the street of otherwise white neighborhoods.

Greco-Persian Wars

❧ The Greco-Persian Wars were a series of wars between Persia and Greece, which started in 499 B.C.E. and lasted until 449 B.C.E. During the wars, in order to avoid capture and being enslaved, some Greek naval crews would run their ships ashore, ignite them, and flee. One crew did this in 490 B.C.E. without realizing how far they were from home and had to walk some 250 miles (400 km) to get back to Athens.

❧ The origins of the marathon are found in the Greco-Persian Wars. Following the defeat of the Persians by the Athenians in the Battle of Marathon in 490 B.C.E., a messenger was sent to run from Marathon to Athens to deliver the news of their victory. The marathon itself was first introduced as an Olympic sport at the 1896 Athens Olympics and the official distance is 26 miles and 385 yards (42 km).

❧ The Hellespont (now known as the Dardanelles) is a stretch of water about 4,000-feet (1,200-m) wide between Greece and Persia. Xerxes (519–465 B.C.E.), the king of Persia, decided to build a bridge here for his troops to cross. However, a storm blew in and the bridge collapsed, causing Xerxes to fly into a rage. He beat the sea with 300 lashes of his whip and threw iron shackles into the water as punishment. Some stories even say that torturers went in with burning brands.

❧ The name of Xerxes' elite fighting force of 10,000 men was "The Immortals." They were so called because every soldier killed was immediately replaced so that the total number was always 10,000.

G

🐦 King Leonidas I of Sparta (circa 540–480 B.C.E.) set out to face Xerxes in battle in 480 B.C.E. with only 300 men. It is estimated that Xerxes' numbers were between 80,000 and 290,000. However, on the first two days of battle the Spartans were quite successful. They proceeded to build a wall out of the bodies of the slain Persians to the horror of the next wave of Persian soldiers that came after them.

🐦 Pausanius, despite being a great Spartan general, decided to betray Sparta and Greece to Xerxes. The Greeks caught wind of this and tried to arrest Pausanius, but he fled and hid in a temple, claiming they could not kill him because he was on sacred ground. So what did they do? They just bricked him in and let him starve to death instead. Easy!

Guevara, Che

 Guevara (1928–1967) studied medicine in Buenos Aires before he became the iconic figure who led the Cuban revolution. Che himself was actually Argentinian while his family was half Irish. His father's real name was Ernesto Lynch.

 Heavy breathing … Che suffered from asthma.

 Time magazine deemed him as one of the 100 most influential people of the twentieth century while Alberto Korta's legendary photograph of Che, entitled *Guerrillero Heroico*, taken when Che was 31 years old, has been called, "the most famous photograph in the world."

 As a young man, Che earned the name *Chancho*, which translates as pig, because of his poor bathing habits. In fact, he proudly changed his shirt only once a week.

 After his execution, Che's hands were amputated. Bolivian army officers transported his body to an undisclosed location, while his hands were preserved in formaldehyde to be sent to Buenos Aires for fingerprint identification.

Gulag

◈ The Gulag population was 30,000 in 1928 and soared to 8 million in 10 years. And where do you put all of these prisoners? The Soviet Union's solution came in the form of "gulags," a series of prison labor camps where detainees tried to redeem themselves through hard labor. In over 476 separate camps it is estimated that 14 million people passed through the gulag system with about 1.5 million dying (but there are no exact statistics). The major industrial cities of the Russian Arctic including Norilsk, Vorkuta, and Magadan were themselves once prison camps run by ex-prisoners.

◈ From 1930–1960, the Gulag administration was the largest single employer in all of Europe.

◈ Alexander Solzhenitsyn, the writer and historian who was awarded the Nobel Prize in Literature in 1970, served as a Soviet artillery officer in World War II and was honored for his courage. In 1945, he was punished for criticizing Stalin in a letter and spent the following eight years in the Gulag as a result.

◈ *Dancing Under the Red Star* by Karl Tobien is an account of a young American girl named Margaret Werner who moved to Russia right before the start of Stalin's terror. She is the only American woman who survived the Gulag to tell her story.

G

Gulf War

❧ The Persian Gulf War occured between August 2, 1990 and February 28, 1991. The war was fought against Iraq, waged by a UN-coalition force of 34 nations and led by the US and UK.

❧ Roughly one in four of the 697,000 U.S. veterans of the 1990–91 Gulf War suffer from Gulf War Syndrome. This condition identified as the likely consequence of exposure to toxic substances, such as pesticides.

❧ The war has the least number of combat casualties since the Revolutionary War with just 84 troops killed in action and 45 more deaths from accidents and other causes. The bitter irony is that so many are going to suffer Gulf War Syndrone the rest of their life instead of having died.

❧ A total of 27,243 Bronze Stars were awarded to Army soldiers for their actions in the Gulf War. A Bronze Star medal represents "heroic or meritorious achievement or service … in connection with military operations against an armed enemy."

❧ 88,500 tons of bombs were dropped on Iraq in 1991, destroying electric, water, and sewage plants.

❧ In 2006, A Gulf War veteran killed four members of his family on a hot evening. David Bradley shot his uncle, aunt, and cousins in the head at close range before walking into a police station. He started the violence after he began to feel tired from the heat.

✎ During the Gulf War, Jacksonville, Florida, had the busiest military port in the country. The military moved more supplies and people from this port than anywhere else in the nation.

✎ In the movie *Three Kings* (1999), several soldiers drink something that looks like mouthwash. During the war, Saudi Arabia's Islamic-based ban on alcohol forced soldiers to find creative ways to import their pleasures. In this case, they had friends and family from home send them vodka tinted with blue food coloring.

Gun Powder

✤ The Chinese invented gunpowder named "Black Powder." The earliest records of its manufacture date back to 850 C.E.

✤ In 1596, Guido Fawkes (1570–1606), an expert with gunpowder, was persuaded by Robert Catesby, leader of the Catholic team plotting to blow up British parliament and King James I of England in London, to help with the scheme. This became known as The Gunpowder Plot and the English celebrate the anniversary of the day the plotters were caught by, among other things, setting off fireworks.

✤ The first use of gunpowder in China for military purposes was in 919 C.E. It reached Europe in the thirteenth century.

✤ Gunpowder is made up of three chemicals: 75 percent potassium nitrate, 10 percent sulfur, and 15 percent carbon.

Gutenberg, Johannes

❧ Johannes Gutenberg (1400–1468) printed the world's very first Bible in Mainz, Germany, in 1456.

❧ The invention of the printing press provided ordinary people with access to the holy book, previously reserved for clergy and nobility.

❧ Legal records show that he was involved in a partnership to produce metal hand mirrors used by pilgrims visiting holy sites. The skills acquired in this endeavor must have been useful to him as he developed a method of making metal type for printing.

❧ Gutenberg revolutionized the distribution of knowledge by making it possible to produce a large number of copies of a single work in a relatively short space of time. For this reason, Gutenberg was proclaimed the "Man of the Millennium" by *Time* magazine in 1997.

G

❧ Roughly 50 of the 200 original Gutenberg Bibles survive today.

Hadrian's Wall

🐦 Hadrian's Wall was built along the English and Scottish border by the Roman emperor Hadrian (76–138). It was meant to keep the Picts and Scottish invaders out of England. The mighty wall spans 73 miles (120 km) across England. Sadly, the whole undertaking was a bit of a waste of time, because the invaders simply paid the Roman guards to let them in.

🐦 Not only was the wall intended to provide security against invaders, but it also prompted the issuance of passports for the first time in history. The document proved citizenship of its people, but more importantly, acknowledged them as tax payers.

🐦 The work was carried out by members of the second, sixth, and twentieth legions. Each legion was 5,000 strong with a work force of up to 15,000.

🐦 Stone was used to first construct the eastern 42 miles (68 km) of the wall, while the 31 miles (50 km) of the western section was initially built using turf in order to hasten the completion of the barrier. Parts of the turf wall were eventually replaced with stone.

🐦 Inscriptions, known as centurial stones, have been detected at intervals of the wall and suggest that each century was allocated a portion of the wall to build.

H

Hannibal of Carthage

❧ Hannibal of Carthage (248–183 B.C.E.) was considered one of greatest leaders and military strategists of all time. Hannibal led his tens of thousands of troops representing parts of Carthage's allies and about 40 war elephants across the Alps in the Second Punic War (218–202 B.C.E.) against the Roman Republic.

❧ Hannibal means "joy of Baal." His family name Barca means "lightning." Barca is also spelled Barcas, Barca, and Barak.

❧ In 184 B.C.E., Hannibal served as commander of the Bithynian fleet in the battle between King Eumenes II of Pergamon (died 159 B.C.E.) and King Prusias I of Bithynia in Asia Minor (228–182 B.C.E.). Hannibal used catapults to hurl pots filled with poisonous snakes into the enemy ships.

❧ In 183 B.C.E., Hannibal committed suicide by taking poison, rather than allow himself to be handed over to the Romans. When he called for the poison, he was quoted to say "Let us relieve the Romans from the anxiety they have so long experienced, since they think it tries their patience too much to wait for an old man's death."

H

Hare Krishna

❧ Established in America in 1965, the Hare Krishna is a popular name for the International Society of Consciousness (or ISKCON) and a religious movement based on Hinduism.

❧ Some Hindus believe that failing to celebrate Krishna's birthday will cause one to be reborn as a snake.

❧ A true Hare Krishna follower heeds a strict diet without intoxicants, stimulants, meat, fish, and eggs, as well as avoiding gambling and sexual relations for pleasure.

H

❧ Hindus in Britain forced the British department store House of Fraser to withdraw an advertising campaign, which they found offensive. The ad featured a small procession of Hare Krishna followers, and said "If I wasn't a chanting, cymbal-banging [sic], easily-led nutcase, who's been brainwashed by some looney [sic] religious sect, I could be wearing Linea Direction's extra fine Merino sweater and linen jeans."

❧ The 16-word mantra "Hare Krishna, Hare Krishna, Krishna Krishna, Hare Hare, Hare Rama, Hare Rama, Rama Rama, Hare Hare," is recommended as the easiest method for self-realization in the present age.

❧ Krishna is a Sanskrit name of God meaning "all attractive," and Rama is another name meaning "reservoir of pleasure."

Hinduism

◦ The Hindu Temple complex known as Angkor is the largest religious building in the world. It's located in Cambodia rather than India.

◦ According to Hindu tradition, the task of cutting one's hair and cleaning the bathroom should be conducted by the "Untouchables," who were considered the lowest members of society and too unclean to touch.

◦ Symbols such as a sacred flame are used to worship God.

◦ *Avatar* is a Hindu word meaning "to come down." The Hindu god Vishnu takes on different forms, or avatars, and descends to the Earth to protect good and destroy evil.

◦ Cow dung may not be the most pleasant object to have in the home, but it has proven antiseptic qualities and medicinal value. Hindus use the dung to clean their homes and purify temples before times of worship.

◦ The *Kama Sutra* is the earliest surviving example of a Hindu love manual. A pop-up version called The *Kama Sutra of Vatsyayana* was published in 2003.

H

Hirohito, Iro

▶ Iro Hirohito (1901–1989) was Japan's 124th emperor and longest reigning monarch, having reigned 63 of his 87 years of life. His subjects believed he was a descendant of Amaterasu, a sun goddess who created the Japanese archipelago from the drops of water that fell from her spear.

▶ In 1915 Hirohito was tutored by Kimmochi Saionju, the former prime minister of Japan.

▶ Hirohito was responsible for one of the worst massacres in modern times. Between December 1937 and March 1938, Japanese troops invaded the Chinese city of Nanjing and embarked on a campaign of murder, rape, and looting. Many women and children were among the 250,000–300,000 people to be killed.

▶ Hirohito narrowly escaped assassination by a grenade thrown by a Korean independence activist, Lee Bong-chang in Tokyo on January 9, 1932.

▶ He was very interested in marine biology and published numerous scholarly works in this field. When he died in 1989, Hirohito was buried with a microscope and a Mickey Mouse watch.

H

Hitler, Adolf

- School reports described the young Hitler (1889–1945) as lazy, disobedient, and rude.

- Benito Mussolini (1883–1945) admitted in 1935 that he was pleased that Hitler carried out a revolution on the same lines as his party, but then added, "They are Germans, so they will end up ruining our idea."

- Hitler joined the Bavarian army serving as a message runner, dashing across the battlefield under fire, carrying orders for officers when World War I (1914–18) broke out in August 1914. In the course of four years, he took part in nearly 40 battles.

- During the final days of the war in 1945, Hitler married his long-time mistress Eva Braun. Less than 24 hours later, the two committed suicide.

- Hitler's great, great grandmother was a Jewish maid.

- Adolf Hitler was fascinated by hands. His library contained pictures and drawings of hands belonging to famous people throughout history.

- In 1938, Hitler was voted man of the year by *Time* Magazine.

- It's been confirmed: Hitler had only one testicle.

H

Ho Chi Minh

- Communist revolutionary leader Ho Chi Minh (1890–1969) was prime minister of Vietnam from 1946–1955. He led the Vietnamese nationalist movement for more than three decades. First he fought against the Japanese, the French colonial occupation, and finally the U.S.-backed South Vietnamese.

- He had reportedly lived in England once and trained as a pastry chef under Georges Auguste Escoffier, the man who developed and revolutionized modern French cuisine.

- The name Ho Chi Minh means "Bringer of Light."

H

- In 1919, he petitioned the powers at the Versailles peace talks for equal rights in Indochina.

- He was a founding member of the French communist party.

- The former capital of South Vietnam, Saigon, was renamed Hô Chí Minh City in his honor.

Hundred Years' War

~❧ The Hundred Year's War between France and England actually lasted 116 years, from 1337–1453.

~❧ The war introduced new weapons such as the English longbow, which could pierce metal and meant that knights were no longer safe, even in full suits of armor.

~❧ All of the battles of the Hundred Years' War were fought in France.

~❧ To counteract the high price of war, European monarchs imposed even more taxes on the people. The French were most adept at this: there were taxes on salt, bread, and wine as well as taxes on the rights to use wine presses, grindstones, and mills.

~❧ No formal treaty was ever signed to end the war.

H

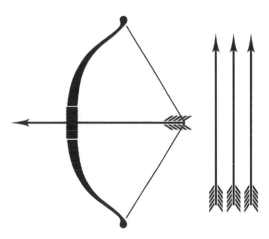

Hungarian Revolution

- The Hungarians' loathing of Russian Communism under which they lived, and the death of Joseph Stalin (1878–1953) led to the Hungarian Revolution (1956).

- There were riots of students, workers, and soldiers who smashed up the statue of Stalin and attacked the ÁVH (the Hungarian Secret Police) and Russian soldiers.

- During the revolution, men who were known to be part of the ÁVH were lynched in public in front of large crowds in Budapest.

- During this uprising, 30,000 people were killed in Budapest alone and about 200,000 Hungarians sought political asylum in the West. Over the next five years, thousands were executed or imprisoned.

- Radio Free Europe and the Voice of America, during this time, encouraged resistance to communist oppression.

H

Inca Empire

🌢 Food for thought? The Inca Empire formed in 1438 C.E. and was the largest civilization in pre-Columbian America. They had sophisticated techniques for storing and preserving food. They freeze-dried potatoes and other tubers by setting them out in dry days and cold nights.

🌢 The Incas built fortresses on the top of mountains that allowed them to see their enemies from afar. One of the most famous was Sacasahuman.

🌢 In spite of not having access to the wheel, the Incas constructed a sophisticated road system to connect villages. They were paved with flat stones and barriers to protect the *chasqui* (messengers) from falling down the side of the cliff.

🌢 Peak performance. The highest point of each village was closest to the sun and reserved for religious purposes.

🌢 What does the gay community and the ancient South American civilization have in common? The rainbow flag. The flags are nearly identical with the exception of an additional blue stripe on the Incan flag.

🌢 In the Inca Empire, knotted cords called *quipu* were used to retain records. Different types of knots, positions of knots, and colors of cords were used to measure population and production.

India

- In all of India's 100,000 year history, it has never invaded another country.

- The Kumbh Mela (Grand Pitcher Festival) is a huge Hindu religious festival in which millions make a pilgrimage to the Ganges River. The full festival only takes place every 12 years and 2001 saw the largest gathering of people in history ever, with some 60 million in attendance.

- The Taj Mahal is a mausoleum in Agra India. It was built by the Murghal emperor Shah Jahan as a tribute to his wife. When it was built the pillars surrounding Taj Mahal were tilted slightly outward so that in the event of an earthquake, they would fall away from the tomb. Building work started in 1632, and finished 22 years later. The emperor also ordered to chop off the hands of the workers who had constructed the Taj Mahal so no one could make anything like it.

- Cows are considered sacred in India and can often be found wandering the streets freely. This is because, like mothers, cows offer milk and can feed the people.

- The earliest cotton in the world was spun and woven in India and was so soft that Roman emperors would call it "woven winds."

- India boasts the largest postal network in the world with some 150,000 post offices. However, it can still take a letter two weeks to travel just 30 miles (48 km).

Indonesia

🐦 Human history in Indonesia goes back at least 1.5–1.8 million years as proved by the fossils of "Java Man," a *Homo erectus* discovered in 1891.

🐦 In 1965 General Suharto, the Head of Special Forces, came to power after an alleged communist coup attempt. The bloodshed that accompanied his rise in power resulted in half a million people slaughtered within a few months.

🐦 In the seventh century, the Buddhist kingdom of Srivijaya made up much of Indonesia until 1290, when it was conquered by the Hindu Majapahit Empire from Java.

🐦 The Portuguese took control of parts of Indonesia in the sixteenth century, but were no match for the much stronger and wealthier Dutch who took on the spice trade in 1602.

🐦 Indonesia is made up of 17,000 islands, but only an estimated 6,000 are inhabited.

🐦 Petal power … The largest single flower in the world is the giant rafflesia, which can span up to 3 feet (1 m) across.

I

Indus Civilization

↬ The Indus civilization was a Bronze Age society that spread across Pakistan, India, and parts of Afghanistan between 2600 and 1900 B.C.E. They had large and complex hill citadels, housing palaces, granaries, and baths that were probably used for sacred ceremonies.

↬ Grain was the basis of the economy and large grain stores collected grain as tax.

↬ Every house had its own courtyard, supply of water (wells), and bathroom. They even had garbage shoots. Trash was disposed of through a slit cut into the house, which would then fall into containers lined up on the street.

I

↬ The Indus region was home to four of the largest ancient urban civilizations, namely Egypt, Mesopotamia, South Asia, and China. The archeological remains were first discovered in the 1920s.

↬ The script of the Indus civilization is made up of a short string of symbols and has never been deciphered.

Industrial Revolution

❧ The Industrial Revolution started in England around 1733 with the first cotton mill. The new inventions that were created led to the development of factories, but as England wanted to keep their technology a secret, they forbid factory workers to leave the country.

❧ An apprentice in an English cotton factory started the Industrial Revolution in America. Samuel Slater (1768–1835) disguised himself and came to America. Here, he reconstructed a cotton-spinning machine from memory.

❧ Today, some countries in Asia and Africa still haven't experienced an industrial revolution and have not made the transition to the Modern Age. These countries are often referred to as "third-world."

❧ Robert Fulton (1765–1815) was the first American to build a steam-powered engine. The engine was used to power steamboats, which became the fastest way of transportation for Americans.

❧ In 1799, the Combination Act made it illegal for two or more factory workers to get together to demand better work conditions and higher pay. Anyone caught breaking the law would be jailed for three months.

❧ Some of the inventions of the Industial Revolution included the sewing machine by Elias Howe (1844), the telephone by Alexander Graham Bell (1876), the electric motor by Nikola Tesla (1879), and the diesel engine by Rudolph Diesel (1892). In 1913, carmaker Henry Ford perfected the process of mass production with his new assembly line.

Iron Age

❧ The Iron Age was a prehistoric period, often identified as starting in Anatolia around 1200 B.C.E. when people learned how to create cutting tools and weapons from iron or steel. The adoption of this material coincided with other changes in society, including differing agricultural practices, religious beliefs, and artistic styles.

❧ Bronze was far too prized in the ancient world to be used for cooking, so it was not until the Iron Age that cooking with metal pots and implements flourished.

❧ Meteorites were the source of iron that were used by prehistoric people.

❧ The oldest known article of iron shaped by hammering is a dagger. It was found in Egypt and was made before 1350 B.C.E.

I

Islam

🌙 Meat that is slaughtered in accordance with Islamic custom is called *zabihah*.

🌙 While Muslims believe that Muhammad and other prophets were important, they do not worship him. When Muslims talk about the prophets, the words "'peace be upon him" are added after their names.

🌙 People or animals are never depicted on prayer mats.

🌙 Islam is one of the fastest growing religions in the world. To become Muslim, a person of any race or culture must say a simple statement, the *shahadah*, that bears witness to the belief in the One God and that Prophet Muhammad was the last prophet of God.

🌙 Islam means "peace through the submission to God."

🌙 Though it may come as a surprise, the majority of Muslims live outside the Middle East. In fact, the most populous country is Indonesia with 184 million muslims.

🌙 The Koran refers to man being equal to woman. The word "man" appears as many times as the word "woman."

Jainism

- Jainism is an ancient Indian religion, which teaches that the way to personal freedom and happiness is to live a life of of harmlessness and renunciation.

- Jains do not believe in the existence of gods or spiritual beings who help human beings.

- The principle of Jain living is nonviolence, also known as *ahimsa*.

- Some Jain monks fast for months at a time, following the example of Mahavira, who is said to have fasted for more than six months. Sri Sahaj Muni Maharaj fasted for a record-breaking 365 days.

- Jains believe in sexual abstinence after the marriage has yielded a son.

- Receiving immunizations, eating meat, lighting fires, digging in the ground, and eating after sundown are all banned in Jainism.

Jewish Diaspora

- The Jewish Diaspora began in 587 B.C.E. when the Babylonians conquered the kingdom of Judea, destroyed the temple in Jerusalem, and exiled a large part of the Jewish population to Babylonia (now southern Iraq). Since then, many of the Jews have lived in exile, commonly called the diaspora.

- The Jewish dispersion has led Jewish settlement in countries across the world including Morocco, Cuba, Mexico, and Australia. There are about 13 million Jews in the world with more than eight million in the diaspora and the remaining five million in Israel.

- The unique displays of the Nahum Goldmann Museum of the Jewish diaspora details the Jewish experience from the exile after the destruction of the First Temple 2,600 years ago to the present.

- England was the first European nation to expel the Jews (in 1290 C.E.).

- Spanish Jews accompanied Columbus (1451–1506) on his famous voyage to the New World (1492). They had been forced to convert to Christianity to escape persecution and death during the Inquisition (1478).

- In 1501 Jews were among groups banned from the Indies by Queen Isabella of Spain.

- Today Jews make up one percent of the world's population and roughly two percent of the population of the United States.

Jonestown

- People's Temple charismatic leader Reverend Jim Jones (1931–1978) and most of the 1,000 members of his People's Temple moved to Guyana from San Francisco after an investigation began into the church for tax evasion.

- In 1978, the bodies of 914 people, including 276 children, were discovered in a communal village known as Jonestown in Guyana, South America.

- Most of the dead, who were known as members of the People's Temple Christian Church, drank Kool-Aid laced with cyanide and sedatives.

- People who had left the organization had warned authorities of brutal beatings, murders, and a mass suicide, but nobody believed them.

- Of all the people who committed suicide, 412 were never claimed by relatives and were buried in a mass grave in Oakland, California.

- The name of the psychedelic, 1990s band Brian Jonestown Massacre was inspired by Rolling Stones guitarist Brian Jones as well as the mass-suicide cult. The documentary *Dig!* followed the rivalry and friendship between the founders of The Brian Jonestown Massacre and another band known as The Dandy Warhols.

Judaism

🌢 Despite modern-day conflicts between them, Judaism is the original of the three Abrahamic faiths, which also includes Christianity and Islam.

🌢 Abraham, the father of Judaism, was the first person to teach the idea that there was only one God. Prior to that time people believed in many gods—including Abraham's father who made his living selling idols of various gods.

🌢 Unlike Christianity, which traditionally has a somewhat reserved attitude toward carnal knowledge (owing to "the fall" of Adam and Eve), Judaism actively encourages its followers to get it on and have large families as it was God who commanded his people in the Old Testament to "be fruitful and multiply" (Genesis I:28; 9:1).

🌢 The Jewish wedding ceremony ends with the groom stamping on a glass wrapped in a cloth napkin—meant as a remembrance of the destruction of the Temples in Jerusalem—though many men joke that it actually symbolizes the last time a newly married man will be able to put his foot down.

🌢 Jews are forbidden to eat leavened bread during Passover and an intermediary is needed to ensure proper observation of the holiday. Over the last few years in Israel, an Arab by the name of Mr. Hussein has assisted the Jews by buying all their leavened products for $4,800 (about 20,000 Israeli shekels) for approximately $150 million worth of leavened products. (Technically he could then keep the lot, but the tradition holds that they give him the deposit back at the end of the holiday).

Justinian's Wars

◆ Justinian (483–565 C.E.) was the second emperor of the Eastern Roman Empire and so successful he was also known as Justinian the Great. He was also the last emperor to speak Latin as his first language.

◆ Before Justinian became emperor he married Theodora, an actress 20 years his junior, which was met with much disapproval because actresses tended to have a bad reputation. Justinian and Theodora never had any children.

◆ Justinian himself never actually took part in any of his military campaigns. However this did not stop him from boasting about his successes in his laws and in art.

◆ I predict a riot! One of Justinian's first conflicts was not against an army but an angry mob. Enraged at a rise in taxes, the Nika Riots (532 C.E.) were in fact made up of armed sports clubs who were the fans of the various chariot-racing teams at the Hippodrome. Putting their sporting differences, aside they came together and formed an organized militia which went on to level the city.

◆ When he came to the throne, Justinian inherited a war with the Sassanid Empire (527–532 C.E.). When King Kavadh I of Persia died in 531 C.E., Justinian I concluded an "Eternal Peace" (which cost him 11,000 pounds of gold). It turns out an eternity is only eight years in diplomatic terms, and hostilities kicked off again in a second war with the Sassanid Empire, which ran from 540–562 C.E.

Kennedy, John F.

🦢 JFK (1917–1963) was the 35th President of the United States. He was also the first Catholic and the youngest person to be elected president at that time.

🦢 Not a bad start in life! When JFK turned 21 years of age, his father gave him $1 million.

🦢 Presidential touch of gold? JFK loved spy novels. At a chance encounter during a press conference JFK mentioned to Ian Fleming, author of the James Bond series, how much he enjoyed the books. Shortly afterward book sales soared and were turned in to the *007* series of movies.

🦢 JFK wrote two books, one of which, *Profiles in Courage*, won a Pulitzer Prize, although there was some question about its true authorship. Some say that it was his speechwriter, Ted Sorensen who did most of the work.

🦢 The Nixon-Kennedy debates were the first ever to be televised and the event proved to be a vote winner for JFK.

🦢 Just hours before he was shot, he mentioned to his wife and friends that it would be easy for an assassin to shoot him from a crowd.

🦢 Following the autopsy of JFK, the coroner's office lost the President's brain and Kennedy was buried without it.

🦢 Only after JFK was shot did it become a federal crime to assassinate the President.

K

Kenya

⚬ Kenya's flag is black, red, green, and white with a traditional Masai shield and spears in the center. The black symbolized the people, the red represents blood, the green is natural wealth, and the white represents peace. The shield and spears represent the defense of freedom.

⚬ Kenya was formerly known as British East Africa until it gained independence in 1963 and became a republic in 1964.

⚬ In 2004, Wangari Maathai received the Nobel Prize for Peace for her activism in women's rights, ecology, and democracy. She is the second woman from Africa to win the Nobel Prize.

⚬ Ancient hominoid, or humanlike skulls, dating back two and half million years have been discovered at Lake Turkana in Kenya.

⚬ Archeologists believe that at least three different species of hominoid were roaming the plains of Kenya, but only one evolved into *Homo sapiens*.

Khan, Genghis

❧ There will be blood! Genghis Khan (1162–1227) was the founder and ruler of the Mongol Empire which went on to invade and destroy large parts of Eurasia. Rumor has it that when Genghis was born he was clutching a blood clot in his fist, which was an omen that he was born to be a great leader.

❧ For one of the greatest emperors to ever live, Genghis Khan's real name was actually Temüjin which means "ironworker."

❧ Despite being born in the foothills of Mongolia, it is recorded in *Collected Chronicles* of the Persian historian Rashid-al-Din that Genghis was tall, long-bearded, had green eyes … and was a redhead!

❧ History has made Genghis Khan so famous that today his face and name endorse a range of products, streets, the Mongolian currency, and Mongolia's main international airport. There are even statues of him placed outside the Mongolian parliament. His name has become so commonplace that there have even been discussions about regulating its use.

❧ An international group of genetic scientists found that nearly eight percent of the men living in the former Mongol empire carry the same y-chromosomal lineage. And because the spread of this gene is so prolific, the authors propose that the lineage is likely carried by male-line descendants of Genghis Khan as it is believed he fathered hundreds or even thousands of children as his armies swept across the continent.

K

King, Jr., Martin Luther

❧ Martin Luther King Jr. (1929–1968) was an African-American civil rights activist and clergyman who was actually born Michael King Jr. (named after his father.) During a family holiday in Germany in 1934, King's father found out about the German Protestant Martin Luther (1483–1586) and so changed Michael's name to Martin in honor of the German Protestant.

❧ The day that King was shot he was staying in room 306 at the Lorraine Motel in Memphis—a place that he and the Reverend Ralph Abernathy stayed in so often when they were passing through that it was commonly known as the "King-Abernathy suite."

❧ Musician Ben Branch was due to perform that night at an event which King was attending and he was on the balcony with King on the day he died. Apparently King's last words were: "Ben, make sure you play 'Take My Hand, Precious Lord' in the meeting tonight. Play it real pretty."

❧ Some say that Martin Luther King was not necessarily shot because he was a powerful black man in America, but rather because he was suspected of being a communist.

❧ After King died, the autopsy revealed that even though King was only 39 years old, he had the heart of a 60-year-old man.

❧ And the award goes to …? King! Who was posthumously awarded the Grammy Award for Best Spoken Word Album in 1971 for his *Why I Oppose the War in Vietnam.*

King Tut

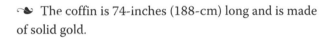

❧ As the most famous pharaoh of Egypt, King Tut (1341–1323 B.C.E.) was only eight years old when he became the king and reigned for nearly ten years.

❧ His remains were left untouched for 3,300 years until Howard Carter discovered his tomb in 1922.

❧ The coffin is 74-inches (188-cm) long and is made of solid gold.

❧ Face value. Tutankhamen's funerary mask is a remarkable example of ancient craftsmanship. Made of gold, it is inlaid with lapis lazuli, cornelian, quartz, obsidian, turquoise, and colored glass.

K

❧ It took more than a decade to catalog, remove, and document the thousands of items found inside his tomb.

❧ Archeologists believe King Tut's wife, Ankhesenamun, was actually his half sister.

❧ Thirty-five model boats were found in Tut's tomb. Two baby mummies were buried in the Treasury. One was a five-month-old fetus.

❧ Lord Carnarvon, the English funder of the dig into King Tut's tomb, died from an infected mosquito bite that led to pneumonia roughly a month after he went into the tomb.

Knighthood

~❧ The origins of the word knight actually mean "boy" or "servant," a somewhat different image of the knight in shining armor!

~❧ The central virtue of a true knight was romantic love—of the non-physical variety of course—along with gallantry, gentility, and generosity.

~❧ Few knights themselves had any title or land. Instead they would just roam around and latch themselves to men with land by either marrying their daughters or by inheriting land from a lord.

~❧ The sons of knights would often begin their training in the art of warfare and chivalry from the age of seven using toy weapons.

~❧ But it wasn't just for boys! The Order of the Hatchet was founded in 1149 by Raymond Berenger, count of Barcelona, to honor the women who fought for the defense of the town of Tortosa against a Moorish attack.

~❧ The two main symbols of knighthood were the shield and spurs. If you were a bad knight you had your spurs hacked off and your shield was hung upside down to show your dishonor.

~❧ Ever wonder why Friday the 13th is unlucky? Some say it is because it was on that date in October, 1307, that Jacques de Molay and 60 of his Knights Templar were arrested in Paris on the orders of King Philip, who felt threatened by their wealth and power.

❧ Mussolini was given an honorary knighthood by Britain in 1923 after he became prime minister of Italy, but it was withdrawn in 1940 as his fascism became apparent and World War II progressed.

❧ Sir Lancelot was considered to be the greatest and most trusted knight of all the Knights of the Round Table in the legends of King Arthur—that is until he slept with Arthur's wife, Guinevere!

❧ The Legend of King Arthur became such a well-known piece of folklore that English King Edward III (1327–1377) even went so far as to create a Round Table just like the one in the story!

Korean War, The

❧ When is a war not a war? Apparently, the Korean War was not really a war, but a military conflict, because the U.S. Congress never actually declared war on North Korea. They regarded it as police action on behalf of a United Nations conflict, though it was one that ended in a stalemate. This is why it is sometimes referred to as "The Unknown War" or the "Forgotten War."

❧ General Douglas MacArthur (1880–1964), who was leading the UN forces in the first part of the Korean War, never spent a single night in Korea, but instead directed his forces from Tokyo.

❧ Phil Day, a soldier from Task Force Smith, which fought one of the first significant battles in the Korean War—the Battle of Osan—is quoted as saying, "We thought the North Koreans would back off once they saw American uniforms."

❧ General MacArthur was relieved from command when, after defeating the North Korean army, he said he wanted to carry on fighting with China. He had actually made it as far as the Chinese border but was pushed back by the Chinese in November 1950. However, MacArthur was fired after he made public announcements to bomb and blockade the Chinese. He also believed that the decision to use nuclear weapons should be his own and not the President's.

K

🐦 By November 30, 1950, the Chinese People's Volunteer Army (PVA) 13th Army Group had managed to expel the U.S. Eighth Army from northwestern Korea. So on December 16, 1950, President Truman (1884–1972) declared a national emergency with the Presidential Proclamation No. 2914, 3 C.F.R. 99 (1953). This remained in force until September 14, 1978, well after the war was over.

🐦 On New Year's Eve 1951, the PVA and the North Korean People's Army (KPA) launched their Third Phase Offensive, also known as the "Chinese New Year's Offensive." Using night attacks, they encircled UN troops and bombarded them with noise from loud trumpets and gongs, in order to disorient them. Being unused to this sort of tactic, some soldiers "bugged out" and fled to the south, leaving their weapons behind.

🐦 The Battle of Pork Chop Hill (March 23–July 16, 1953) was originally designated as Hill 255, but its contour lines on a map of Korea and a 1959 movie on the subject made it world famous as Pork Chop Hill.

🐦 Meanwhile the Battle of Old Baldy (June 26–August 4, 1952) refers to the series of engagements to secure hill 266. It earned the name Old Baldy after artillery and mortar fire destroyed all the trees on its crest.

Ku Klux Klan

🐦 The origins of the name for the Ku Klux Klan are varied but one erroneous version is that it is derived from the onomatopoetic word for the sound of the loading and locking of a bolt-action rifle. The truth is that it most likely originates from the Greek word for circle—"kuklos"—and the word "clan."

🐦 Do you believe in magic? The Grand Imperial Wizard was the title given to the leader of the Reconstruction-era KKK, which existed in the nineteenth century in the U.S. while a "Grand Dragon" was the highest ranking Klansman in a given state.

🐦 IRS as Civil Rights champion? In 1944, the IRS filed a lien for $685,000 in back taxes against the Klan, and the organization was forced to dissolve in 1944 with local Klan groups closing soon afterward.

🐦 During the rise of the second Klan (1915–1944) across the U.S. much of the iconography (including the wearing of white sheets and burning crosses) was not originally inspired by actual klan members, but rather was poached from David Griffith's movie *The Birth of a Nation* (1915), said to have been based on Thomas Dixon's 1905 novel, *The Clansman*.

🐦 Dynamite Hill became the unofficial name of an area known as College Hills in Birmingham, Alabama when, in the late 1940s, the upwardly mobile successful African-American families who lived there were the regular target of white bombers. Similarly Birmingham quickly became known as "Bombingham."

~~ Membership in the Klan is secret, so the Klan has signs that members use to recognize one another. A member may use the acronym *AYAK* (Are you a Klansman?) in conversation to identify himself to another potential member and the response *AKIA* (A Klansman I am) completes the greeting. Not to be confused with IKEA.

~~ Given their unusual name, over the years the Klan have coined many words beginning with "KL," such as Klabee (treasurers), Klavern (local organization), Kleagle (recruiter), Klecktoken (initiation fee), Kligrapp (secretary), Klonvocation (gathering), Kloran (ritual book), Kloreroe (delegate), Kludd (chaplain).

~~ The second clan not only targetted African-Americans but Roman Catholics, Jews, and foreigners. Even bootleggers and divorcees found themselves as targets of the KKK.

~~ The second Klan was also known to have been funded by Nazi Germany when, in 1940, they joined up with the German-American Bund—a group whose purpose was to promote a positive view of Nazi Germany in the U.S.

~~ Even though there was an eye witness to positively identify him and he was found to have 122 sticks of dynamite without a permit, Robert Chambliss, KKK member, was let off with a $100 fine and a six-month jail sentence for the bombing on 16th Street Baptist Church, which killed four young African-American girls in 1963. Eventually, in 1977, he was retried and sentenced to life in prison.

Lee, Robert E.

⚜ Robert E. Lee (1807–1870) was the commanding general of the Confederate Army during the American Civil War (1861–65). The "E" in Robert E. Lee is Edward.

⚜ Lee's most famous horse was called Traveler. He was a large white horse standing nearly 16 hands high. Lee rode him throughout the war though he did own four others horses called Richmond, Lucy Long, Brown-Roan, and Ajax.

⚜ He surrendered to General Ulysses S. Grant at Appomattox Courthouse in Virginia on April 9, 1865. Lee's last words before he died were "Tell Hill he must come up. Strike the tent," according to J. William Jones' *Personal Reminiscences, Anecdotes, and Letters of Gen. Robert E. Lee.* However, given that Lee had suffered a stroke resulting in aphasia (rendering him unable to speak), it is unlikely he was able to say anything at all.

⚜ On September 29, 2007, three of General Lee's Civil War-era letters were sold at auction by Thomas Willcox for $61,000. Willcox had apparently been driving around with the letters in his car for months following a clear out of his parent's house. South Carolina tried to sue Willcox to stop the sale—claiming that the letters were the property of the state—but the court ruled in favor of Willcox.

Lincoln, Abraham

🐦 Abraham Lincoln was the 16th President of the United States. The tallest President so far at the time, standing at six feet four inches (1.9 m) tall, he certainly reached great heights in stature and accomplishments.

🐦 He was also the first U.S. president to have a beard.

🐦 On May 22, 1849, Abraham Lincoln received Patent No. 6469 for a device to lift boats, though the device was never manufactured. However, it did make him the only U.S. president to hold a patent.

🐦 During the American Civil war the king of Siam (now Thailand) offered to send Lincoln elephants to help in the fight. Abe, probably quite sensibly, turned him down.

🐦 Show me the money! Lincoln is credited with creating a national banking system with the National Banking Act of 1863, which resulted in standardizing the U.S. currency.

🐦 Abe was known to suffer from deep depression, a battle which he would fight his whole life. Those closest to him knew of his propensity to weep in public, tell inappropriate stories at odd times just to get a laugh, and as a young man, even threaten suicide.

🐦 Abe Lincoln also held a liquor license and even operated several taverns.

L

Lithuania, Republic of

🐦 Lithuania is a country in northern Europe that is the most southerly of the Baltic states and can be found between Poland and Latvia. So why is this country so special? Well for one, in the fourteenth century it was actually the largest country in Europe! While its present day geography is slightly larger than the state of West Virginia, with a total area of 25,174 square miles (65,200 sq km) at one point Belarus, the Ukraine, parts of Poland and parts of Russia were all part of the Grand Duchy of Lithuania.

🐦 The Grand Duke Gediminas, who is said to have founded the capital, Vilnius, claimed the whole idea came to him in a dream. He dreamt of a wolf letting out a tremendous howl of a thousand wolves from a hilltop and he interpreted it as a sign that he should build a fort there.

🐦 On Christmas Eve in Lithuania it is tradition to serve 12 dishes—one for each apostle—and everyone has to try a little of each or it is deemed bad luck. It is also said in Lithuania that on Christmas Eve animals are able to speak (maybe it's the vodka).

🐦 And who believes in the Easter Bunny? In Lithuania it is the Easter granny—*Velyku Senele*—who brings all the eggs. But she does let the bunnies help her to paint them.

🐦 In Lithuania there are two rather interesting hills: the Hill of Witches and the Hill of Crosses. The former is covered in carvings of pagan gods, animals, and other creatures, the latter (as you would probably guess) is covered in thousands of crosses of all shapes and sizes.

L

Magna Carta

❧ The Magna Carta was a document that King John of England (1166–1216) was forced into signing. It reduced the power he held as a monarch and allowed for the formation of a stronger parliament. The Magna Carta became the basis for English citizen's rights.

❧ The Magna Carta is comprised of multiple documents. The first was sealed in 1215 and the final was issued in 1300. There are 17 surviving versions from the thirteenth century.

❧ The latest chapter in the history of the Magna Carta was sealed by King Edward I (1239–1307). It sold at Sotheby's in New York for 21.3 million dollars.

M

❧ Thomas Jefferson (1743–1826) often referred to the Magna Carta when he addressed English governors and the government of George III.

❧ This most famous English legal document was originally written in Latin. The Magna Carta is Latin for "Great Charter."

❧ Although today's history students remember the date 1215 (which is when King John signed the first official charter), the rights that form part of today's law were from the 1297 adaptation.

❧ The popular fictional character Robin Hood is usually depicted as an enemy of King John.

Malcolm X

- Malcolm X moved on his own to New York when he was 17 and drifted into a life of crime involving hustling, prostitution, and drug dealing. By 19, he was arrested and sentenced to ten years in prison.

- When he was in prison, he picked up a dictionary and copied every entry. It took him a whole day just to write the first page.

- Malcom X once said, "Be peaceful, be courteous, obey the law, respect everyone; but if someone puts his hand on you, send him to the cemetery."

- Spike Lee's biopic *Malcolm X* (1992) won the Silver Berlin Bear Award at the 1993 Berlin Film Festival.

M

- In *The Autobiography of Malcolm X*, Malcolm reports that one of his duties when working as a shoe shiner at the Roseland State Ballroom in Boston was to sell condoms.

- Malcolm was born on May 19. In Berkeley, California this day is a city holiday, Malcolm X Day, where kids are off from school.

- Girl power ... Malcolm X had six children—all girls. The two youngest were twins born after he was killed.

- On February 21, 1965, Malcolm X was gunned down in broad daylight at a political rally at the Audubon Ballroom in Harlem, New York.

Mamluks

❧ The Mamluks were actually a slave army of nomadic Turks from central Asia who were captured as young boys and sold into military slavery. They existed from the ninth to the nineteenth centuries.

❧ The Mamluks spoke their own Turkish language as well as the Arabic of their masters.

❧ In 1250 the last sultan of Saladin's dynasty in Egypt was murdered and a Mamluk general by the name of Aybak took power. But he only ruled until 1257, when his wife had him killed in the bath.

❧ The average reign of a Mamluk ruler in Egypt was seven years.

❧ As the power and authority of the Mamluks began to rise, many free Egyptians would arrange to have themselves sold into slavery in order to gain access to the privileges afforded the Mamluks.

❧ Napoleon (1769–1821) also knew of the Mamluks strength and not only did he form his own Mamluk corps (which became the last known Mamluk force), but his own personal bodyguard, Roustam Raza, was a Mamluk who had been sold in Egypt.

❧ The name Mamluk was also used in Hungary in the late nineteenth century as a nickname for members of parliament there belonging to the governing "Liberal" party.

M

Marxism and Karl Marx

M

🕭 Karl Marx (1818–1883) and Friedrich Engels (1820–1895) were the fathers of the socio-political philosophy that interprets history as a constant struggle between the social classes ... but this came to be known only as Marxism. When Marx and his coauthor Engels fled to London in 1849, the Prussian authorities put pressure on the British government to expel them because their ideologies and several articles they had written were critical of the Prussian government. But Prime Minster Lord John Russell refused, believing it was more important to preserve the right to free speech.

🕭 In 1883, Karl Marx accused his son-in-law Paul Lafargue (a Marxist socialist journalist whose most famous work was entitled *How to be Lazy*) and his friend Jules Guesde of "revolutionary phrase-mongering," which led to the now famous remark, "If that is Marxism, then I am not a Marxist."

🕭 Marx had seven children by his wife Jenny von Westphalen and one illegitimate child with his housekeeper Helene Demuth, who Engels pretended was his own in order to protect Marx's reputation.

🕭 During his time in London, Marx spent a good deal of his time at the British Library reading back issues of *The Economist* to better analyze capitalist society.

❧ Marx and his family were known to be living hand-to-mouth so that he could devote his time to his philosophy. They survived in part thanks to Engels, who would send them postal orders of £1 and £5 notes which were cut in half and mailed in separate envelopes.

❧ Marx's health was so bad that he said to Engels, "such a lousy life is not worth living." Having suffered a bad attack of boils in 1863, Marx also told Engels that his only consolation was that "it was a truly proletarian disease."

❧ Karl Marx, who spent a good portion of his life in Britain, believed that Russia was too backward to ever become communist and that Great Britain would be the first nation to adopt his ideas. He never lived to see how wrong he was!

❧ Are you sitting comfortably? When Marx finally did shuffle off this mortal coil on March 14, 1883, he did so from the comfort of his armchair.

Mary, Queen of Scots

- Mary (1542–1587) was almost 6-feet (1.8-m) tall and beautiful, and she was an excellent dancer and athlete.

- Even though white was regarded as the color of mourning in sixteenth-century France, Mary Stuart insisted on wearing white for her first wedding, to Francis II of France.

- Mary loved horse riding and was known to disguise herself as a stable boy and ride out at night into the streets of Edinburgh.

- Mary had four ladies-in-waiting who were also called Mary: Mary Fleming, Mary Seton, Mary Beaton, and Mary Livingston. Only Mary Seton remained in loyal service to the Queen almost until the bitter end.

M

- When Mary was executed for treason it took three strokes of the axe to sever her head from her body.

- Off with her head! When the executioner lifted Mary's severed head to the crowd, it slipped from his grip and fell to the ground and he was left holding only a wig. By the end of her days Mary's hair was quite gray and very short.

- After the execution it was revealed that her little Skye terrier, who was Mary's companion during her last years in prison, had hidden under her voluminous gown throughout the whole ordeal.

Mary I of England

🐦 The first daughter of Henry VIII and half sister to Elizabeth I and Edward VI, Mary I (1516–1558) was a staunch Catholic. She earned herself the name of "Bloody Mary" for the fact that she had hundreds of religious dissenters burned at the stake during her reign in the Marian Persecutions.

🐦 The recipe for a Bloody Mary is as follows (from the New York School of Bartending):

1 shot of vodka in a highball glass with ice
fill with tomato juice
a pinch of celery salt
a pinch of ground black pepper
a dash of Tabasco
2–4 dashes Worcester sauce
1/2 tsp horseradish
a dash of lemon or lime
Garnish with a celery stalk

M

🐦 Mary was a sickly child who suffered from bad headaches and stomach aches. As a grown woman, because she struggled to bear children physicians said she had what was known at the time as "strangulation of the womb."

🐦 Mary used to send cucumbers from her garden to her stepmother Jane Seymour while she was pregnant with the future Edward VI to help satisfy Jane's pregnancy cravings.

❧ On July 25, 1554, Mary was wed to Philip II of Spain at Winchester Cathedral, just two days after their first meeting.

❧ The nursery rhyme "Mary, Mary, Quite Contrary" is often equated with Mary I:

> Mary, Mary, quite contrary,
> How does your garden grow?
> With silver bells, and cockle shells,
> And pretty maids all in a row.

❧ The reference to "contrariness" referred to her attempt to revert a Protestant England to Catholicism. The query about the growth of her garden was a jibe at her infertility. The silver bells to represent the Catholic church, while the pretty maids refer to her miscarriages, or the fact that she had Lady Jane Grey executed for ascending the throne after the death of Edward VI. It is interesting to note that this nursery rhyme has also been linked to Mary, Queen of Scots, for similar reasons: the garden was the reign of her realm; the silver bells representing the Catholic church; the cockle shells a poke at her husband's infidelity; and the pretty maids referring to the Four Marys, her laides in waiting.

Mayan Civilization

❧ On a blue note ... The color Maya Blue is an azure blue pigment. which was used by the Mayans. It was made from indigo dyes and mixed with leaves from the Añil plant and with clay.

❧ Mayan civilization existed in pre-Columbian Mexico and Central America from about 2000–250 B.C.E. For the Mayans, Venus was the most important astronomical object—even more so than the Sun.

❧ The Mayans liked to practice human sacrifices and in some rituals, people were killed by having a priest cut the person's chest open and tear out his heart as an offering.

❧ According to Mayan mythology which is recorded in the *Popol Vuh* (*Book of the Council)*, the first ancestors of the Mayans were made from maize dough.

M

❧ The Mayans desired some unusual physical characteristics for their children. While they were still young, boards were pressed onto babies' foreheads to create a flattened face. Another practice was to cross babies' eyes by dangling objects in front of them until they became permanently cross-eyed.

❧ Doctor! Doctor! The Mayans were innovative surgeons and were known to suture wounds with human hair and were able to reduce fractures. They even made great dentists, making prostheses from jade or turquoise, and filling teeth with iron pyrite.

The Mayans were also one of the first civilizations to develop the calendar, although it only had 260 days. The calendar itself was divided up into 20 divisions of 13 days, and each day had a special name from a list of 20. The calendar itself was used to determine the correct time for religious and ceremonial events.

Time's up! Many people believe that according to the Mayan Long-count Calendar, the world will end on December 21, 2012.

Mecca

🐦 Mecca, which can be found in modern day Saudi Arabia, is the most holy place in Islam and during the Hajj pilgrimage, muslims are required to come and walk around the Sacred Ka'bah (a cube-shaped structure) seven times.

🐦 Before the advent of Islam, Mecca used to be a place of pilgrimage for pagans who visited the Ka'bah, which they filled with idols. The main business of Mecca before Islam was trade, and caravans came from across the land to buy and sell goods.

🐦 Nowadays, Mecca is a place of pilgrimage for all Muslims, and *only* Muslims can enter the city.

🐦 Mecca has in the past been called a "relay station" for cholera in its spread from East to West. Back in the day, Mecca was regularly afflicted by cholera epidemics and 27 outbreaks have been recorded during pilgrimages between 1831 and 1930. During the Hajj of 1907–08 some 20,000 pilgrims are said to have died.

🐦 Risky business! It may be a place of pilgrimage, but it is also fraught with danger partly due to the number of people descending on the city at one time. For example, on April 9, 1998, 118 people died in a stampede; on April 15, 1997, 217 were killed and 1,290 injured in a fire; on May 23, 1994, 270 were killed in a stampede; and on July 2, 1990, 1,426 were killed when a tunnel collapsed.

M

Medieval Europe/Middle Ages

- The Battle of Bosworth (England 1485) was important as it is not only the battle that marked the end of the Middle Ages, but it was the last to use a mounted charge of knights and the last one in which an English king, Richard III, died on the battlefield.

- The world's first universities were established in Europe during the Medieval period in the 1100s. Oxford University in England was one in particular that had to make a rule to forbid students from bringing bows and arrows to class.

M

- Under Medieval law even animals could be tried and sentenced for crimes. Records exist of farm animals being tried for injuring or killing people, including mice who were taken to court for stealing part of a harvest, and flocks of locusts convicted—in absentia—of eating crops.

- The word quarantine dates back to fourteenth-century medieval Europe when Venice decreed that ships should be isolated in the harbor for 40 days (or *quarantina* in Italian) to allow for any possible manifestation of the plague on board those ships to present itself.

- Before the development of the Carolingian Miniscule (a writing standard) in the ninth century, ancient and medieval scripts were written in a continuous stream of character with no spaces. It took until the fifteenth century to develop punctuation marks.

Medieval Music

❧ For weddings and on Valentine's Day, musicians would play buoyant and cheery music with crescendos, which were known as "chivarees."

❧ Medieval music was played on a variety of instruments including recorders, horns, trumpets, whistles, bells, and drums.

❧ On May Day, a specicially written, high-pitched piece of music would be played to awaken the hibernating spirits and forewarn the arrival of spring.

❧ Not only was the music played for enjoyment, it also supposedly aided in the digestion of food.

❧ Do-re-medieval ... Early Medieval music was first played in unison. The notes were generally of the same length and played in the key of C major. Harmony was gradually integrated and by the twelfth century, a method of music notation was developed to indicate the length of notes and pitch.

❧ The gemshorn, an early recorder made from animal horns, was likely used by shepherds to comfort their herds.

❧ The "Gregorian Chant," the name for unaccompanied Latin text sung in unison during the Roman Catholic mass, was named for Pope Gregory I.

❧ Troubadors were among the few literate people in the Middle Ages.

M

Mesopotamia

- Mesopotamia (roughly 3000–1500 B.C.E.) was the area in and around the Tigris-Euphrates river system (which is now modern-day Iraq) and also parts of northeastern Syria, southeastern Turkey, and southwestern Iran. It is significant as the society credited with inventing the wheel, the plow, irrigation systems, and the sailboat.

- Mesopotamian religion did not include a heaven or hell, but rather taught that when a person died they would go underground as a ghost and eat dirt.

- What's for dinner? If the priests wanted to know what the gods desired, they would read the livers of chicken or lambs they had sacrificed for their answers.

M

- Mesopotamian science and mathematics were based on a sexagesimal (base 60) numeral system which is the source of our modern-day 60-minute hour, 24-hour day, and 360-degree circle.

- The Baghdad Battery, which may have been the world's first battery, was created in Mesopotamia during the later Parthian or Sassanid periods.

◆ If all else fails ... The Mesopotamians were good at treating the symptoms and diseases of a patient by using bandages, creams, and potions. But on the odd occasion when a patient could not be cured, Babylonian physicians liked to use exorcism to cleanse the patient of any curses.

◆ The main gods in Mesopotamian religion were earth, water, air, and the heavens. But just in case that wasn't enough they also had some 3,000 lesser gods for everyday needs.

Mexican Revolution

➤ The Mexican Revolution began in 1910 and ended around 1920, the result of frustration on the part of Mexicans toward President Porfiro Diaz (1830–1915). On becoming a dictator, he suppressed any political opposition and bullied the electorate into voting for him. In the end Alvaro Obregon became president of Mexico in 1920, though he started out in life as a chickpea farmer.

➤ José Doroteo Arango Arámbula (also known as Francisco "Pancho" Villa) (1878–1923) was one of the leading figures in the Mexican Revolution. He led the Mexican revolt against the U.S., and never drank alcohol. He allowed his men to drink, but he didn't touch the stuff until after he negotiated peace with Alvaro Obregon in 1920.

M

➤ Pancho Villa's career as a revolutionary leader began after he fled to the mountains following the shooting of the man who had raped his sister. Making good money as a bandit, Pancho was known to give some of it to the poor and this, in turn, gave him the moniker as the Robin Hood of Mexico.

➤ Pancho Villa had a reputation for ruthlessness and was known to have killed many men on and off the battlefield. But when a task was too gruesome for even him to handle he fortunately had Rodolfo Fierro—who was known to be loyal, fearless … and a sociopath! He once shot a man dead just to see if he would fall backward or forward. *Ay Caramba*.

Ming Dynasty

🐦 The Ming Dynasty ruled China from 1338 to 1644. The name "Ming" means brightness and was chosen by the first Ming Emperor Zhu Yuanzhang Hongwu (1368–1398) as a contrast to the dark period in which the dynasty came to power.

🐦 Zhu Yuanzhang was not like other Ming emperors because he came from a poor family in which his parents and most of his siblings died from either plague or starvation.

🐦 During the Ming Dynasty, the Forbidden City (in modern-day Beijing) was built. It took more than 200,000 workmen to handle the construction between 1407 and 1420. There are 9,999 rooms (including the antechambers) and because the buildings are made of wood, giant cauldrons of water were placed throughout the complex as a safeguard.

M

🐦 The bristle toothbrush, similar to the type used today, was invented in China during the Ming Dynasty in 1498.

🐦 The deadliest earthquake of all time occurred during the reign of Emperor Zhu Houcong Jiajing in 1556. Approximately 830,000 people were killed in the region of Shaanxi.

🐦 Inventor Song Yingxing (1587–1666) was responsible for documenting a wide range of technologies which further developed the Ming Dynasty—including snorkeling gear for pearl divers.

Mongols

🐚 Founded by Genghis Khan (1162–1227) in 1206, the Mongol Empire was the largest continuous land empire in history. At its height it stretched over 12,800,000 square miles.

🐚 Kublai Khan (1215–1294), the grandson of Genghis conquered China and established the Chinese Yuan Dynasty (1271–1368).

🐚 Paper chase … Italian traveler and explorer Marco Polo discovered the use of paper currency in the Mongol Empire.

🐚 She wears the pants … In his travel writings, Marco Polo remarked on the habit of gentrified women in the Mongol-ruled province of Badakhshan to wear trousers.

M

🐚 Mongols traditionally drink salty tea. Sometimes they also add milk, butter, and flour to the mix.

🐚 Genghis Khan believed in freedom of religion. His name means "oceanlike ruler." Archeologists have never been able to locate his secret tomb.

🐚 On average Mongol children learned to ride bareback on a horse by the age of four.

🐚 Both Kublai Khan and his father were the fourth sons of their families.

Mussolini, Benito

❖ Benito Mussolini (1883–1945) became the fascist dictator of Italy in 1922, but before his rise to power he was qualified to be an elementary school teacher. In a desperate bid to avoid military service as a young man, Mussolini moved to Lausanne, Switzerland, in 1902 where he was arrested for vagrancy.

❖ Benito Andrea Amilcare Mussolini was in fact named after Benito Juarez—a Mexican president—because his father was a staunch socialist. Mussolini's middle names are also a tribute to the Italian socialists Andrea Costa and Amilcare Cipriani.

❖ Mussolini apparently had a favorite drink, which was a strawberry sherbet frappé, made with strawberry sherbet, Chianti wine, and angostura bitters. This was so well known among Italians that when—near the end of World War II—a man named Giuseppe Marscone ordered the drink in a bar he was lynched by an angry, anti-Mussolini mob.

❖ Mussolini was also an avid soccer fan and more than 50 years after his death, the Lazio team still suffer image problems because they were the dictator's favorite team. This has not been helped by the fact that at the beginning of the twenty-first century, roughly 30 percent of the team was owned by the National Alliance, an extreme neo-fascist party.

❖ Despite their alliance during World War II, Mussolini and Adolf Hitler did not get along and Mussolini found it hard to be civil to him, referring to Hitler as a dangerous buffoon and calling him, "the new Genghis Khan."

M

Napoleon I and the Napoleonic Era

— ✥ —

N

❧ Napoleon (1769–1821) was a military and political leader who rose up to become the emperor of France. His policies had a deep impact on European politics in the nineteenth century and beyond.

❧ After the Battle of Friedland on June 14, 1807, Napoleon agreed to meet his opponent, the Russian Czar Alexander I, to discuss how best to carve up Europe. Neither would set foot on the other's territory, but there was a door of opportunity. They agreed to meet in the middle on the Neman River in Eastern Europe in an elaborate room built on a raft with a door on either side for the emperors to enter.

❧ Feline uneasy? Apparently Napoleon suffered from ailurophobia, which is a fear of cats. Ironic that there now exists a breed of cat called the Napoleon, which has short legs and a Persian face.

❧ After the French Revolution, Napoleon removed Leonardo da Vinci's *Mona Lisa* from the Louvre to have it hang on the wall of his bedroom.

❧ A real pain the …! Napoleon's final defeat was at the Battle of Waterloo (June 18, 1815) and his lack of success is believed to have been caused by his hemorrhoids! Finding it too painful to ride his horse out to oversee the troops, he delayed his attack as the weather got worse—giving the British and Prussians the advantage.

Native Americans

⤙ The fabled saber-toothed tigers (Smilodon) that early North American settlers would have come across were actually just large feral cats.

⤙ Native American people used to use Buffalo tails as fly swatters.

⤙ When Omaha Indians divorced, the woman got the property and kids.

⤙ The state name "Iowa" comes from the Sioux word meaning both "one who puts to sleep" and "beautiful land". "North Dakota" comes from the Sioux word for "friend."

N

⤙ Dartmouth College in Hanover, New Hampshire was founded by Eleazar Wheelock in 1769 primarily to educate Native American people. The college's charter issued by King George III describes its mission as "the education and instruction of Youth of the Indian Tribes in this Land … and also of English Youth and any others."

⤙ Stink bugs! The Delewares used skunk oil to treat colds.

⤙ Knock on wood … The tallest totem pole was 180 feet, 3 inches (54 m) tall, and was made in 1994 in British Columbia.

⤙ Pocahontas (circa 1595–1617) was only 10 or 11 years old when she saved the settler John Smith from execution.

Nazi Party

🙢 The National Socialist German Workers' Party was a political party that existed in Germany from 1919 until the end of World War II in 1945. The term "Nazi" was actually coined by the journalist Konrad Heiden and it was meant to be a derogatory term. The party members had originally called themselves "Nasos" because it was an abbreviation of National Socialist.

🙢 In the same way that the Prussian kings and emperors historically wore black uniforms with skull-and-crossed-bones badges, the Nazis also sported uniforms with skulls on them. Many of those uniforms were made by Hugo Boss.

N 🙢 Starting in 1936, all German boys aged 15 to 18 had to join the Nazi Party Youth Organization where they had to pass such tests as running 50 meters in 12 seconds, going on two-day hikes, and memorizing various nationalistic anthems. Once you passed you were rewarded with a knife that had the words "Blood and Honor" carved in the handle.

🙢 Senior Nazi Hermann Goering apparently disliked the regulation toilet paper so much that he bought large supplies of soft white handkerchiefs to use instead.

🙢 The famous Nazi motivational rallies were inspired by Harvard cheerleaders. Ernst Hanfstaengl, a close comrade of Hitler said he passed on the idea after having studied at the Ivy League university, and that the inspiration for the shout "Sieg Heil!" came from the cheerleaders' routines.

Nightingale, Florence

❧ Florence Nightingale (1820–1910) nursed the care of thousands of soldiers during the Crimean War (1853–56) and was known affectionately as the "Lady with the Lamp."

❧ She devoted her life to campaigning for health reform and to nursing. Second to Queen Victoria, she was the most influential woman during Victoria's reign. Nurses really do call the shots.

❧ "Let experience, not theory, decide upon this as upon all other things," she was once quoted as saying.

❧ Three hospitals in Istanbul, Turkey, have been named after her.

❧ Nightingale's 1859 volume *Notes on Nursing* was intended for use by home nurses.

❧ Florence called herself "a man of action."

❧ The Thirty-third Derby Beer Festival, which took place in Derbyshire, England chose the "Lady with the Lamp" as the festival's 2010 theme.

❧ The Florence Nightingale Syndrome refers to the phenomenon of a nurse working so intimately with a patient that she/he falls in love with him or her. The effect was explored in the 1985 movie *Back to the Future.*

N

Nuremberg Trials

- After World War II, the Allies conducted what became known as the Nuremberg Trials—a series of military tribunals to try the leaders of Nazi Germany for their war crimes. The trials were held in Nuremberg because there were no prisons that could be used in Berlin.

- The trials were held in the Palace of Justice, the very same building where in 1935 the Jews were demoted to second-class citizens.

- The chief prosecutor at the Nuremberg Trials was Robert "Justice" Jackson who had doubts about how successful the trials would actually be. They turned out to be the basis on which international law operates today.

- During the trial, an atrocity movie introduced by the Russians was shown, but was loaded into the projector upside down, causing much laughter in the courtroom.

- Rudolf Hess, who was tried for acting as Adolf Hitler's Deputy in the Nazi Party, spent most of his time during the trial reading books.

- Don't shoot the messenger! British Army officer Airey Neave was the man tasked with serving the war crime indictments to the accused in their cells during the trials and as a result met many of the most infamous German war criminals. He was killed by a car bomb set up by the Irish National Liberation Army in 1979.

❧ Ernst Kaltenbrunner was known as "The Man Without a Signature" after claiming complete ignorance of the atrocities during World War II despite being presented with evidence of documents (with his signature), which proved the opposite.

❧ Three men who were found guilty and sentenced to death—Wilhelm Keitel, Alfred Jodl, and Hermann Goering—asked to be shot rather than hanged. They were, though Goering in the end committed suicide with a cyanide pill just hours before his execution.

Old North Bridge

- Paul Revere (1735–1818) of the famed "midnight ride" to warn colonists that the British Army was advancing, was a dentist as well as a silversmith. He first paddled across the Charles River before jumping on the horse that would take him ultimately to Concord, where the historical battle would take place the following day at the Old North Bridge. After shots at Lexington, this marked the beginning of the Revolutionary War.

- Supposedly Paul forgot his spurs as he went galloping off to warn the colonists about the oncoming British.

- The Minute Men, members of the colonial volunteer militia who fought the British troops, ranged from age 16 to 60.

- The North Bridge has been rebuilt five times since 1775. The current bridge was built in 1956 and restored in 1995.

- The bridge spans the Concord River, a body of water about which author Henry David Thoreau wrote in his first book: *A Week on the Concord and Merrimac Rivers* (1849).

- Although the Battle of Concord fought at this site is remembered in stories as the start of the Revolutionary War, the first shots were actually fired in nearby Lexington, Massachusetts.

Opium Wars

❖ The British began trading opium with the Chinese because they did not want to keep handing over silver currency for goods. Over time, British exports of opium from India to China grew from an estimated 15 tons in 1730 to 75 tons in 1773. The product was shipped in more than 2,000 chests, each containing about 140 pounds (64 kg) of opium. By the 1820s China was importing 900 tons of Bengali opium annually.

❖ High times! By the 1820s, enough opium was getting into China to sustain the habits of around a million addicts.

❖ In March 1839 the Chinese Commissioner Lin Zexu ordered the British merchants to hand over all of their opium stocks within three days and to sign an agreement pledging never again to traffic in the drug under penalty of execution. The Brits, under the orders of Superintendent of Trade, Charles Elliott, eventually conceded. Lin then washed an estimated 20,000 crates of opium into the sea.

❖ Opium was not illegal in England at this time, and prior to the 1868 Pharmacy Act restricting the sale of opium to professional pharmacists, anyone could legally buy and trade opium.

❖ The style of smoking opium in a pipe may have become popular as a result of the craze for tobacco smoking, which started in the Qing dynasty.

❖ Chinese smokers, if caught, could be punished with 100 blows of the bamboo and forced to wear a heavy wooden collar for a month or more.

O

Ottoman Empire

- The Ottoman Empire was a regime that lasted from 1299 to 1923 and at points encompassed areas as far and wide as southeastern Europe, western Asia, and North Africa.

- Not only was Suleiman I (aka His Imperial Majesty Grand Sultan, Commander of the Faithful and Successor of the Prophet of the Lord of the Universe) the longest reigning Sultan in the Ottoman Empire, but he was also a distinguished poet and goldsmith.

- Meanwhile Sultan Selim—Sultan from 1512–1520—introduced the policy of fratricide—the murder of brothers. Under this system, as soon as the Sultan had produced his first son, all his own brothers and their sons would be killed. The Sultan's own sons would then be confined until their father's death, at which point the whole system would start all over again. In the later centuries, the Sultans resorted to imprisonment rather than execution for their brothers.

- The Sultanate of Women was 130-year period during the sixteenth and seventeenth centuries when the women of the Imperial Harem exercised tremendous political influence because their sons were minors and too young to rule the empire. Many of these women were born as Christians and became some of the most famous European and Greek Muslims.

- The Tulip period in Ottoman history was a peaceful time from 1718–1730 when the Ottoman court went crazy for tulips. They not only cultivated them but incorporated them into arts and textiles.

Parks, Rosa

🍂 Rosa Parks (1913–2005) rose to fame on December 1, 1955, for refusing to give up her seat on a bus to a white passenger, leading to the Montgomery Bus Boycott, which lasted 382 days. It was one of the most successful mass protests against American racial segregation.

🍂 The bus on which Rosa Parks ended up making her stand was the number 2857 Cleveland Avenue bus.

🍂 The vehicle itself was a General Motors transit bus with the serial number 1132 and it is now an exhibit at the Henry Ford Museum in Dearborn, Michigan.

🍂 On December 8, 1955, Parks faced trial and in a hearing lasting 30 minutes was found guilty of violating a local ordinance. The fine was $10 plus a $4 court fee.

🍂 Although Rosa Parks was born in 1913, she only received her high school diploma in 1934.

🍂 Hey you! In 1999, a lawsuit was filed against the hip-hop group Outkast and its label because they had used Rosa Parks' name in their song "Rosa Parks" without her permission.

🍂 Rosa Parks was the first woman and second African-American to be laid in state at the U.S. Capital Rotunda in Washington D.C. after her death.

P

Pearl Harbor

❧ One of the nicknames for Pearl Harbor is "Gibraltar of the Pacific."

❧ You snooze, you lose in life in this case. Because the Japanese planned their attack early on Sunday morning, many of the soldiers were sleeping and not necessarily at their posts to defend the harbor.

❧ In 2007 (66 years after the explosion that destroyed *Arizona)* it was determined that a U.S. quart of oil still leaked from the hull and rose to the surface of the water each day.

❧ At the time of the bombing of Pearl Harbor, the top U.S. Navy command was called CINCUS, which was pronounced "sink us." This was soon changed for PR purposes.

❧ Only one Japanese soldier was actually arrested during the attack on Pearl Harbor. Kazuo Sakamaki swam ashore after his submarine was grounded and was captured.

❧ In case there is any doubt … A declaration of war on the part of the Japanese was printed on the front page of Japan's newspapers in the evening edition of December 8, 1941, but an *actual* declaration of war was not delivered to the U.S. government until the day after the attack.

P

Peloponnesian War, The

❧ It's showtime! The Peloponnesian War (431–404 B.C.E.) was fought between the Athenians and the Spartans. It lasted so long that most of Aristophanes comedies written during this period satirized many of the generals and political figures of the time.

❧ The Spartans had a reputation for being tough. Children were forced into physical fitness at a young age and at birth they belonged to the state of Sparta instead of their parents. If they looked weak when they were born they were left on top of a mountain to die. At seven they were sent off to join a "herd" of their own peers to battle out who would be the leader of the other children. At 12 years of age they were given a cloak to wear but were only allowed to bathe a few times a year. They were kept hungry and encouraged to steal food because this taught them stealth on the battlefield.

❧ One of the key generals during the Peloponnesian War was named Pericles, who insisted he should always be portrayed in art and sculpture wearing a helmet because he didn't want people to see that he was bald.

❧ Alcibiades, an Athenian general, was a desperate attention seeker. On one occasion he cut off the tail of his favorite dog just to get people to notice him.

P

❧ During the battle against the Spartans at Syracuse in Sicily (415–413 B.C.E.) the same Alcibiades decided to deface some of the statues of the gods by knocking off their genitalia. Rather than head back to Athens and face the music for his sacrilegious act, Alcibiades decided to give up the secrets of the Athenian army to the Spartans instead. Still, he didn't meet a happy end. The Spartans killed him once they had the tip off.

❧ When you play with fire, someone's gonna get burned. The Greek army from Boetia were the first to develop the flame thrower when they sacked the city of Dellum (circa 424 B.C.E.).

❧ At the Siege of Megara in Athens (circa 431 B.C.E.), the locals allegedly found an ingenious way to fight off their attackers who were mounted on elephants. They doused a dozen pigs in oil and set them alight to frighten off the pachyderms.

❧ And how does it end? After having waited for four days for the Spartan's to move their ships into battle at Hellespont, the Athenian Commander Conon had little choice but to beach his ships so that the soldiers could search for food on land, their supplies having run very low. It was then that the Spartans struck and victory was theirs.

Peron, Eva

🕊 Eva Peron (1919–1952) was a Taurus.

🕊 Although Eva acquired the nickname "Little Eva" (Evita), she was not particularly little, at 5 feet 5-inches (1.6-m) tall.

🕊 Eva was born out of wedlock and destroyed her birth certificate so there would be no documentation.

🕊 She once played the part of Queen Elizabeth I of England in a historical radio drama.

🕊 Sixteen people were killed when the public went to pay their respects to Eva Peron who died in 1952 at the age of 33.

🕊 Madonna won the role of Evita in the 1994 biopic after writing a letter to the director Alan Parker. Madge speaks only 140 words in the entire movie, the rest was sung.

P

Peter the Great

- Peter I or Pyotr Alexeyevich Romanov (1672–1725) was czar and emperor of Russia and was responsible for modernizing the empire and making it a significant European power. But before he could get started, Peter first had to share it with his sickly brother Ivan V, his half-sister Sophia acting as regent. The "co-czars" worked together until Ivan's death from natural causes in 1696.

- In the battle against the Turks in 1695, Peter actually fought as a regular foot soldier among the troops.

- Peter was six feet, seven-inches (2-m) tall, and it is said that he also suffered from epilepsy.

- Hair today, gone tomorrow … In his desire to westernize Russia and bring it in line with Europe, Peter forbade the wearing of beards. He would not only cut off the beards of his own noblemen, he also charged a tax for those who continued to wear a beard.

- Peter's first marriage to Eudoxia Lopukhina was not a match made in heaven and resulted in the birth of a single child, Alexei. Eventually Peter had his wife exiled to a monastery and the marriage ended in divorce.

- Peter is said to have married his mistress, Catherine, in secret in 1707 before marrying her publicly in 1712. He later made her co-ruler and they had 11 children, though only two survived into adulthood.

Phoenicia and the Phoenicians

❧ Phoenicia was an ancient civilization that existed at the east end of the Mediterranean Sea (1550–300 B.C.E). The Phoenicians were responsible for the expansion of maritime trading culture across the Mediterranean. They were so good at traveling by sea that according to legend, the Egyptian pharaoh, Necho II, hired a band of Phoenicians to map and circumnavigate the coast of Africa, which they did in three years.

❧ By roughly 1200 B.C.E, the Phoenicians had developed symbols which were to become the foundations of the modern-day alphabet. Consisting of just 22 consonants, each with its own sound, the symbol of the ox head was called aleph or "a" and the symbol for house was beth or "b." When the Greeks got their hands on it, aleph became alpha and beth became beta—hence alphabet.

❧ Ever wonder why purple is often associated with royalty? From as early as the eighteenth century B.C.E. it was the Phoenicians who mastered the art of extracting the dye, a few drops at a time, from the *Murex* sea-snail's shell. Because the process was so difficult and time consuming, only the rich could afford it, leading to the expression "born in purple" for those who are born into wealth.

❧ The Greeks learned a great deal about naval navigation from the Phoenicians, who taught them to sail using the North Star as a guide.

P

Pillar Dollar

- The pillar dollar was the currency minted in the New World by the Spanish Empire from 1732 and got its name from the Pillars of Hercules which appeared on the reverse. It is the basis for the modern day U.S. and Canadian dollar, and also the Chinese yuan.

- The pillar dollar was derived from the Spanish dollar, which in turn was also known as a piece of eight or an eight-real coin because it was worth eight Spanish reales.

- The Spanish dollar was meant to correspond to the German *thaler,* which was pronounced "dah-ler" in Low German and this is where we get the term dollar from today.

- Put your money on the line. The pillar dollars were milled exclusively at Potosi, Bolivia; Lima, Peru; and Mexico City, but they were only milled in Mexico City during the reign of Philip V (1683–1746) of Spain.

- A license to print money! Even though the U.S. eventually started manufacturing its own currency following the Coinage Act of 1792, the first U.S. dollars were not as popular as the pillar dollars, which were heavier and made from a better quality of silver. Therefore, these Spanish coins remained legal tender in the U.S. until 1857.

- Pillar dollars from the Mexico City mint could be easily identified from those from other mints by the mark of an M with a small "o" above it.

Pinochet, Augusto

🌰 For crying out loud! Augusto Pinochet (1916–2006) was the dictator and President of Chile from 1973–1990. As a boy, he was described as a sensitive child who cried a lot during scary movies.

🌰 As he grew older, little Augusto seemed disinterested in school and earned such poor grades that he was eventually expelled from San Rafael Seminary for bad behavior.

🌰 Augusto Pinochet's rise to power was very slow (it took some 40 years) and he was regarded as such an apolitical figure that the socialist president, Salvador Allende (1908–1973), himself promoted Pinochet to head of the army, such was his belief in Pinochet's trustworthiness.

🌰 At the start of rule as the head of Chile, Pinochet gave a *carte blanche* to a group of economists known as the "Chicago boys," nicknamed because of their devotion to University of Chicago economist Milton Friedman's freemarket theories.

🌰 Despite the disappearance of 3,428 persons (according to the Rettig Report) and the torture of 27,255 persons (according to the Valech Report) during his time in power, Pinochet was so confident about his public support in Chile that he called a plebiscite for the 1988 general election vowing he would step down from the presidency if he failed to secure the public's confidence. He lost and stepped down in 1990.

P

🐦 Augusto Pinochet had a variety of nicknames depending on whether you supported or opposed him. Supporters called him *mi general* (my general) while his opponents called him *pinocho* (Pinocchio).

🐦 Before the coup that Pinochet led to oust President Allende, he allegedly said to him, "President, be aware I am ready to lay down my life in defence of the constitutional government that you represent."

🐦 Will that be cash or charge? In 2004, a U.S. money-laundering investigation uncovered that Pinochet and his associates had 125 securities and bank accounts dating back 25 years through which they had secretly moved millions of dollars.

🐦 In 1998, Pinochet was recovering from back surgery in London when he was arrested on an international warrant calling for his extradition to face charges of murder of a number of Spanish nationals who had died during his regime.

🐦 In July 2002, all charges against General Pinochet were dropped, after the Chilean Supreme Court upheld a ruling that he was mentally unfit to stand trial.

Pirates

❧ Argh! Shiver me timbers! The term "buccaneer" is generally synonymous with pirates these days, but the origins of the word come from the French *boucanier* or, "someone who smokes meat," which is exactly what pirates had to do in order to get enough rations on board the ships for their long journeys.

❧ Captain Morgan (1635–1688) is not just the name of some rum. He was also a pirate and Welshman who not only went on to be Governor of Jamaica, but was also knighted.

❧ William Dampier (1652–1715) was no ordinary buccaneer, but also a best-selling English author, a naturalist, a mapmaker, and a botanist. His travels gave us such words as chopsticks, barbeque, and avocado.

❧ Pirating was obviously such a lucrative business that governments wanted a piece of the action—so they created privateers. These men behaved exactly like pirates in terms of looting, pillaging, and attacking other ships, but would do so under the direction of their home countries against an enemy state. However, once the wars were over these privateers usually went back to "illegal" pirating.

❧ Captain William Kidd (1645–1701) was a Scottish pirate who was caught and found guilty of murder and piracy. On May 23, 1701, he was hung at Execution Dock in Wapping, London, but the rope broke and he had to be hung twice. His body was then left to hang in an iron cage over the River Thames for the next 20 years as a warning to all other pirates.

P

🖢 Welshman Black Bart (1682–1722) only became a pirate after the ship he was commanding was attacked and seized by pirates. But then he went on to break all records for piracy himself by capturing the most ships and stealing the most money in the course of his career.

🖢 The infamous English pirate, Blackbeard (1680–1718) started his career during the War of Spanish Succession (1701–1714) going to sea at an early age and serving on an English ship, which played a role in Queen Anne's war, privateering against the Spanish in the Spanish West Indies and along the Spanish Main.

🖢 Not just for the boys! There were female pirates too, such as Anne Bonny, Mary Read, Grace O'Malley, Charlotte de Berry, Jane de Belleville, and, from China, Ching Shih. All of them were just as ruthless as the men they sailed with.

Plymouth Rock

🐦 In 1741, 94-year-old Thomas Faunce, the town record keeper thought he had identified the rock where the first pilgrims allegedly set foot. Turns out he was wrong. The pilgrams actually first landed in what is now Provincetown, Cape Cod, MA.

🐦 In 1774, the inhabitants on Plymouth were off their rocks when they decided to move the boulder to a shrine. But when it was lifted it split in two, and half of the rock was left behind on the wharf. Some viewed the split as a symbolic omen of a division with the British Empire.

🐦 It is estimated that the rock left behind in the harbor once weighed as much 20,000 lb (9,000 kg) before souvenir hunters chipped away at it.

🐦 Today, the visible portion of Plymouth Rock is a lumpy fragment of glacial moraine that is about the size of a coffee table.

🐦 Just in case the rock goes missing, there is one more piece in the Patent Building in the Smithsonian.

🐦 In 1920, Plymouth Rock was temporarily relocated so that the old wharves could be removed and the waterfront redeveloped.

🐦 Plymouth Rock has been ceremoniously buried twice by Native American rights activists. The first in 1970 and again in 1995 as a part of the National Day of Mourning protests.

P

Polo, Marco

❧ Friends in high places! Italian Marco Polo (1254–1324) traveled to China with his father when he was a boy and became a hit with the then Mongolian ruler Kublai Khan (1215–1294).

❧ The exact date of Marco Polo's death is unknown because Venetian law states that the day ends not at midnight, but at sunset. So his death is somewhere between January 8 and 9, 1324.

❧ Marco Polo spoke four languages in addition to his native Latin and they were Uighur, Persian, Chinese, and Mongolian.

❧ Marco Polo was from Venice, so the airport in that city is named after him. But it is Hong Kong's airline, Cathay Pacific, that has named their frequent flyer program the "Marco Polo Club."

❧ There is also a subspecies of sheep (*Ovis aries*) nicknamed the Marco Polo sheep. The animal can be found in the mountainous regions of Central Asia and is distinguished by its large size and spiraling horns—the longest of any sheep.

❧ In the 2008 video game *Civilization Revolution*, Marco Polo makes an appearance as a Great Explorer.

Pompeii

~⚬≫~

~⚬ ...nt Roman city that was buried by a volcanic
eru... s (79 C.E.) and was only discovered 2,000 years
late... ...ied bread that had been baking on the day of
the ... ...vens.

~⚬ The citizens of the ancient city of Pompeii, like fellow countrymen of
the Roman Empire, cleaned clothes in urine.

~⚬ The rich living in Pompeii had murals on their walls painted to look
like natural landscapes.

~⚬ Birds ceased their chirping on the morning of August 24, 79 C.E., the
day Mount Vesuvius buried the city in ash.

~⚬ Pliny the Younger (61–112 C.E.), whose eyewitness account of the
eruption that destroyed Pompeii survives to this day, owned a Villa named
"Tragedy."

~⚬ Plaster of Paris was used to make casts of the victims of the volcano,
both of people and animals. The shapes of the corpses were in some cases
perfectly maintained by cavities in the ash.

~⚬ Since the 1970s, nearly 600 items have been stolen from Pompeii.

~⚬ Around midnight on August 25 the cloud that erupted from the
explosion had reached approximately 20 miles (32 km) high.

P

❧ The House of the Vettii is one of the most famous houses in Pompeii. Named possibly after its owners, the Vettii brothers, the house contained signet rings that were discovered during an excavation. The garden was adorned with marble and bronze statues—12 of them were fountainheads that spouted water into a series of basins.

❧ Thirty-three bakeries have so far been discovered in Pompeii.

❧ Pompeii is considered one of the 100 most endangered cultural sites according to the World Monuments Fund. Pollution has caused stone structures to crumble and frescoes to fade.

❧ Ashes to ashes ... Though archeologists have dedicated hundreds of years to uncovering the site, one-third of the city still lies buried.

Pope Alexander VI

🐦 Spanish Pope Alexander VI was the pope from 1492 until his death in 1501 and is renowned as one of the most corrupt and secular popes of the Renaissance.

🐦 He was no saint. He fathered at least seven children with a number of mistresses. His most famous offspring were his son Cesare who murdered political rivals and his daughter Lucrezia who was married off to a number of men for political gain.

🐦 He was in constant need of money to support his lavish lifestyle and accepted many political bribes.

🐦 He was so unpopular that when he died at the age of 72, the priests of St. Peter's Basilica initially refused to accept his body for burial.

🐦 His successor, Italian Pius III who became pope from 1503, refused to give permission for a mass for Alexander to take place, stating that it was, "blasphemous to pray for the damned."

P

Popes

❧ The Pope's title of *Pontifex Maximus* actually means "supreme bridge builder" and was a title formally held by the pagan high priests of Rome.

❧ Like father, like son! Hormisdas was pope from 514 to 523, and his son Silverius, held the position in 536. He didn't last quite as long as his father, and was only 17 months on the job.

❧ Pope-elect Stephen was only pope for three days—from roughly March 22/23 to March 25/26, 752 C.E., dying of apoplexy before he could even be consecrated.

❧ The 94th pope, Paul I, who held the position from 757–767, was the first pope to succeed his own brother, Pope Stephen II.

❧ Pope Adrian II (pope from 867 to 872) was the last married pope. He refused to renounce his marriage and his daughter, so his family lived in the Vatican with him.

❧ Due to an administrative error there was no Pope John XX. Pope John XIX was pope from 1024–32 and the next John to be pope was Pope John XXI from 1276–77.

❧ Pope Clement VII was pope from 1523 until he ate a poisonous deathcap mushroom in 1534 and died.

❧ The 146th pope, Benedict IX (pope from 1032–1045), was the only person to become pope more than once (three times to be precise).

Prime Ministers

❧ Earl Grey tea, a tea blend that uses bergamot oil, is named after a British prime minister named Charles Grey, 2nd Earl Grey. He was prime minister from 1830–34.

❧ Leaving it a bit late? Henry John Temple, 3rd Viscount Palmerston was prime minister from 1855–1865 and was the oldest to first take the office at 70 years of age. He also avoided rushing into wedlock, and only got married for the first time at the age of 55, in 1839. The blushing bride? His mistress Emily, Lady Cowper.

❧ Andrew Bonar Law was prime minister of Britain from 1922–23 but he was not even British. In fact, he was a Canadian and the shortest-serving British prime minister of the twentieth century having only spent 211 days in office.

❧ Sir Charles Tupper was prime minister of Canada from May 1 to July 8, 1896, and holds the record for the shortest time in office, at only 68 days.

❧ And who were The Ramrods? Apparently they were an Australian rock band that was once managed by Paul Keating, who was prime minister of Australia from 1991–96.

P

Presidential Assassinations

- Missing the missus … Mrs. William McKinley was not present at the funeral of President William McKinley.

- Members of the Secret Service were riding in a 1955 Cadillac convertible behind the President's limousine on November 22, 1963.

- Lincoln's son, Robert Todd Lincoln, was at his father's deathbed, though not present at the shooting. He was at the train station where President James Garfield was killed and at the Pan-American Exposition in Buffalo when President McKinley was shot.

- Of Lincoln's four sons, only Robert lived to adulthood. Bizarrely, John Wilkes Booth's brother, Edwin, rescued Robert when he fell between a train and a platform in Jersey City, New Jersey not long before President Lincoln was asassinated by John Wilkes Booth.

- The Secretary of Agriculture is the ninth person to be called upon should the President, Vice President, Speaker of the House, etc., be unable to fulfill their duties.

- When he was shot, Abraham Lincoln and his wife were watching the play, *Our American Cousin* at Ford's Theatre in Washington D.C.

❧ The myriad drawings of a mortally wounded Lincoln lying in a bed across the street from the Ford's Theater are inaccurate in this way— Lincoln was so tall he had to be laid on a diagonal.

❧ Charles J. Guiteau, a mentally disturbed government-office seeker, shot James Garfield on July 2, 1881. The president did not actually die from the gunshot wound, but from blood poisoning after 16 different physicians attempted to treat him.

❧ On January 30, 1835, President Andrew Jackson was attending a funeral for a congressman when a gunman named Richard Lawrence attempted to shoot him with two different derringers. Both misfired.

❧ Three weeks before the presidential election in 1912, Theodore Roosevelt was shot in the chest by a deranged saloonkeeper from New York while delivering a speech in Milwaukee. He was saved by a folded 50-page speech and a metal glasses case that were in his coat pocket.

❧ Two assassination attempts were made on President Gerard Ford ... both by women.

Prohibition

- Prohibition in the U.S. was the period in which the manufacture, transportation, import, export, and sale of alcohol was prohibited. Some towns were so convinced that the banning of alcohol would end almost all crime, they actually sold their jails.

- Temperance activists (those who were against the use of alcohol) even hired scholars to rewrite the Bible, taking out any and all references to alcohol.

- Some prohibitionists were in favor of some rather extreme measures to dissuade others from taking to the drink, including the distribution of poisoned alcohol through bootleggers.

P

- Meanwhile the term "speakeasy" got its name because one had to whisper a code or a name through a hole in a door to gain access to premises selling illegal booze.

- The term "bathtub gin" got its name not because it was mixed in a tub necessarily, but because the large bottles and jugs used to mix the alcohol, glycerine, and juniper juice were too big to fill with ordinary kitchen faucets and had to be filled by the bathroom faucet.

- Some people were so desperate for a drink during Prohibition that they even fell for the urban myth that if you filtered antifreeze through a loaf of bread, the alcohol was then safe to drink! Many died as a result.

Protestantism and the Protestant Reformation

❖ The Protestant Reformation and the rise of Protestantism was the result of various individuals across Europe challenging the authority of the Roman Catholic church and its dogma. English theologian John Wycliffe (1324–1384) was one of the first. A lay preacher and founder of the Lollard Movement, and his criticism of the Roman Catholic church in the fourteenth century earned him the nickname the "Morning Star" of the Reformation.

❖ The term Lollard came from the Dutch word for mumbler and was used to decribe the religious radicals in continental Europe at that time.

❖ After Wycliffe's death from natural causes, Pope Martin V ordered that Wycliffe be posthumously exhumed, and burned as a heretic—in 1428—some 44 years after he had died.

❖ Jan Hus (1369–1415) was a professor at the University of Prague who became the leader of the Czech reformation and died a martyr when he was burned at the stake. Jan Hus Day on July 6 is still a public holiday in the Czech Republic even though today few Czechs describe themselves as religious, and the few that do are Roman Catholic.

P

❧ German Martin Luther (1483–1546), an Augustinian friar who was critical of the Roman Catholic church's practice of indulgences (paying the church for forgiveness from God), was known to suffer from kidney stones. He self-medicated with a late medieval remedy called *dreckapotheke*—a cure made from human and animal excrement.

❧ Ever try a Diet of Worms? It's not just any old diet! In the fifteenth century, diets were the name for general assemblies of the Imperial Estates of the Holy Roman Empire, and Worms is one of the oldest cities in Germany. The Diet of Worms (28 January to 25 May 1521) was the meeting at which Martin Luther was eventually excommunicated from the Roman Catholic church because he refused to recant his challenges.

❧ The Affair of the Placards (October 17, 1534) was an incident in which anti-Catholic posters were erected overnight in cities across France—one was even nailed to the door of King Francis I bedchamber at Ambroise.

Prussia

🐦 Prussia is the historical region and former kingdom of north-central Europe that included present-day northern Germany and Poland and at its peak stretched from The Netherlands and Belgium in the west to Lithuania in the east. Its greatest importance was in the eighteenth and nineteenth centuries when it exercised considerable power in Europe. Prussians have often been described as authoritarian, militaristic, and very orderly, an image which came about from observation of the unswerving obedience of the Prussian army.

🐦 The Prussian King Friedrick Wilhelm I (1713–1740), aka "the Soldier King", was responsible for building up the Prussian army. He had a particular fetish for tall men and so put together an army of towering troops. One of his regiments was known as the Potsdam Giants, whose minimum requirements were that the men be at least 6 Prussian feet (about 6 feet 2 inches or 1.9 meters) in height. The king is even quoted as saying: "The most beautiful girl or woman in the world would be a matter of indifference to me, but tall soldiers—they are my weakness."

🐦 Nice try! During the Franco-Prussian War (July 19, 1870–May 10, 1871), the Prussians managed to seize Paris. So, the French came up with an ingenious plan. Léon Gambetta, minister of the interior in the new French government, escaped from the city in a hot air balloon and regrouped the French army in the countryside. The Prussians still won.

P

✒ Charge it! It was during the Franco-Prussian War that the last major cavalry charge was used in Western Europe. On August 16, 1870, at Mars-la-Tour, the Prussians were struggling to gain the upper hand. The "Von Bredow's Death Ride" was a successful cavalry charge where the Prussians used terrain and gun smoke to mask their movements from the French until the very last moment, coming into view just 3,300 feet (1,000 m) from the French lines.

✒ The real man of steel! Otto von Bismarck (1815–1898) was also known as the Iron Chancellor for his strong-arm tactics and pragmatic approach to politics. Not only did he work under three Prussian kings, but was prime minister of Prussia and played a large role in unifying Germany.

Qin Dynasty

꙳ꙮꙮ

꙳ The Qin (pronounced "chin") Dynasty (221–206 B.C.E.) was the first ruling dynasty of Imperial China and is the dynasty from which modern-day China gets its name!

꙳ Qin up … For a dynasty that lasted only 12 years, the Qin Dynasty was the first to standardize the Chinese language as well as establish weights and measures and to introduce the use of currency.

꙳ After having defeated all members of the previous Zhou dynasty (1046–221 B.C.E.), Ying Zheng decided he should have a name to suit his new position, so he had it changed to Qin Shihuang Di, which means "First Emperor of the Qin."

Q

꙳ During his reign as emperor (246–221 B.C.E.), Qin exercised extreme censorship, persecuted scholars, and destroyed all books that did not deal with topics of medicine, agriculture, or prophecy. He had all the "useless" books burned and as for the 400-odd scholars who refused to hand over their books? They were either buried alive or sent to work on the Great Wall of China.

꙳ Perhaps not surprisingly then, three attempts were made on Qin Shihuang Di's life.

꙳ Ruling in the current world was not enough for Qin, he wanted to make sure he had an army fit for an emperor in the afterlife. So had the Terracota Army of Xi'an built (dating from 210 B.C.E.), with some 8,000 soldiers, 130 chariots with 520 horses, and 150 cavalry horses. The tomb was found by a local farmer in 1974 when he was drilling for water.

Queen Victoria

❧ Queen Victoria (1819–1901) reigned over the United Kingdom and Ireland for a remarkable 63 years and seven months. She was also the first empress of India for the British Raj. Despite being queen of England, Victoria was actually mostly of German descent. Her first language was German, though she did also speak English, French, and a little Hindustani.

❧ Keep it in the family … Queen Victoria married Prince Albert of Germany, on February 10, 1840. He was her first cousin.

❧ She may not have been the very first to do so, but because she wore a white dress on her wedding day, Victoria started a worldwide trend for brides to wear white when they wed.

❧ Queen Victoria was the first monarch to travel by train and her first voyage was on June 13, 1842 from Slough, near Windsor, to Bishop's Bridge, near Paddington, in London.

❧ To this day, Victoria is known as the Grandmother of Europe—having had nine children with her husband Albert, most of whom then married in to Europe's other royal families.

❧ Queen Victoria's reign is remarkable in that not only is she still the longest-living British monarch but she is the longest-living female monarch in history.

Roman Empire

🐦 Flavious Honorius (384–423 C.E.) was Roman emperor for just two years (393–395 C.E.). He had a favorite chicken named "Rome." This made things a tad confusing when the city itself was overrun by Goths and a messenger told him that "Rome is lost." Hororious panicked until he realized that it was the city and not his prized pet.

🐦 Emperor Heliogabalus (or Eliogabalus) (218–222 C.E.) had an unusual hobby. He liked to collect spiders' webs … by the ton.

🐦 The letters SPQR stand for *Sentus Populus Que Romanus* and the Romans left these tags or trademarks wherever they went. These letters even appear on the drain covers in Rome today and it translates as "The Senate and the Roman People."

🐦 The Roman Empire didn't just bring Roman baths, highways, and plumbing to the rest of western civilization, but they also brought cats, stinging nettles, cabbages, and peas.

🐦 In order to take an oath it was customary for citizens of Ancient Rome to put a hand on their testicles.

R

Roosevelt, Franklin D.

↝ Franklin Delano Roosevelt was the only President elected to four terms (1933–1945).

↝ FDR's mother forced him to wear a dress until he was five years old.

↝ When not in Washington, D.C., FDR had another home away from home. His cottage in Warm Springs, Georgia was called the "Little White House" because he spent so much time there.

↝ A monument to FDR finally unveiled in Washington, D.C. on May 2, 1997, by President Bill Clinton, had been the subject of heated controversy as to whether or not FDR should be shown in his wheelchair. Public pressure led to the inclusion of an exact replica of one of his wheelchairs, created for display in the Memorial Entry Building.

↝ Not only were FDR and Winston Churchill world leaders and great friends, they were also related. FDR was Churchill's seventh cousin, once removed on his mother's side.

↝ FDR was sitting for a portrait by American artist Elizabeth Shoumatoff when he suffered his fatal stroke in April 1945. The portrait was never completed.

↝ FDR was the first American president since Abraham Lincoln to visit troops on the battlefield.

↝ FDR was an avid stamp collector and he pursued this hobby throughout his tenure in office.

Russian Revolutions

❧ Before the Russian Revolution kicked off, the Russian Empire itself covered one-sixth of the land surface of the globe and had a population of almost 150 million from more than a hundred different nationalities.

❧ There were actually two revolutions which took place in 1917. The February Revolution marks the start of the initial worker's protests, but because the Russians used the Julian calendar as opposed to the Gregorian calendar (which at the start of the twentieth century was 13 days behind), the revolution technically started in March.

❧ Germany had a vested interest in destabilizing Imperial Russia prior to the Russian Revolution of 1917, and even helped to ferry home Vladimir Lenin and other antiwar radicals from Switzerland in April 1917.

R

❧ When the royal Romanov family was murdered in July 1918, the incident took place in a basement in the city of Yekaterinburg, central Russia. Speculation abounded that one member of the family may have survived, but DNA testing proved in 2009 that indeed the whole family had been killed by either gunshot or bayonet.

❧ It was only after the Russian Revolution that Finland actually regained its independence, having been under Imperial Russian control since 1809.

Safavid Dynasty

S

- The Safavid Dynasty ruled Iran from about 1501 until 1722 and if you trace back the genealogical line of Ismail I, founder of the Safavid Dynasty, it leads back to Eudokia Palaiologina, who in turn was daughter of Byzantine emperor Michael VIII Palaiologos who in turn is believed to be a descendent of Charlemagne (742–814), King of the Franks and the first Holy Roman Emperor.

- Ismail I's main challenge was to bridge the gap between two opposing factions of the Safavid state. On one side were the Qizilbash (aka the Redheads—derived from their distinctive twelve-gored crimson headwear known as Haydar's Crown) who were the "men of sword" versus the Persian "men of pen" who filled the bureaucracy.

- Shah Ismail II, who reigned from 1576–78, spent 20 years in prison after being accused of plotting to oust one of his father's leading courtiers. By the time he came to power in 1576 he sought revenge by not only executing his opponents, but also killing or blinding members of his own family. The Qizilbash plotted an assassination with the help of Ismail's sister, but he died of an opium overdose instead.

- Shah Abbas I (1587–1629) developed an obsessive fear of assassination, so he put to death or blinded any member of his family he thought might be plotting against him. This included executing one of his sons and blinding the two others, both of whom eventually died before him, leaving Abbas I with no heir.

Salem Witch Trials

-☙ The Salem Witch Trials were the trials of suspected witches that took place in colonial Massachusetts between 1692 and 1693. Following the unexplained "possession" of Betty Parris—daughter of the village minister Samuel Parris—a neighbor by the name of Mary Silbey encouraged their maid, Tituba, to make a cake from the urine of the victim and feed it to the dog. This only drew greater attention to the fact that Tituba could indeed be a witch.

-☙ One explanation for the bizarre convulsions and visions experienced by the victims of the Salem Witch Trials could have been "convulsive ergotism." This would have been brought on by ingesting rye infected with ergot, a fungus that can invade the rye grain, especially under warm and damp conditions. The symptoms of this illness also cause—among other symptoms—fits and hallucinations.

-☙ Dorothy Good (down on record as Dorcas Good) was probably the youngest of those accused of witchcraft to go to jail along with her mother Sarah Good. She was just four years old.

-☙ Present at the hangings of the accused witches was the Reverend Nicholas Noyes who asked of the accused Sarah Good if she would confess. Her reply: "I am no more a witch than you are a wizard, and if you take away my life God will give you blood to drink." It was 25 years later that Reverand Noyes was to meet his maker, dying of a hemorrhage and choking to death on his own blood. Spooky!

S

🐾 Sarah Osborn would become the first victim of the Salem Witch Trials—dying of natural causes while still in jail.

🐾 Even when the trials ended, many of the suspects were stranded in prison because they could not afford to pay for their release. Even though they were under arrest, it was customary for the prisoner to pay for their own food and board.

🐾 Delayed reaction? The state of Massachusetts only got around to apologizing for the Salem Witch Trials in 1957—more than 250 years after the events took place.

Sassanid Empire

🔸 The Sassanid Empire (224–651 C.E.) was the last pre-Islamic Persian Empire, which included the territory of modern-day Iran, Afghanistan, Iraq, and Syria as well as the Caucasus, southwestern Central Asia, parts of Turkey, the Arabian Peninsula, the Persian Gulf, and southwestern Pakistan. It was regarded as one of the two superpowers of late antiquity, along with the Roman Empire and later the East Roman Empire.

🔸 At the time of the death of King Hormizd II, who reigned from 302–309 C.E., there was no immediate heir to the throne. His three sons had either been killed, blinded, or imprisoned. This left the succession to his as yet unborn son, Sharpur II, who was crowned in utero. It was said a crown was placed on his mother's stomach to confirm his birthright. What would they have done if the baby had been born female?

🔸 Shapur III, was the eleventh king of the Sassanid Empire and only reigned for five years, from 383–388 C.E. It is said he met his end after a hurricane blew over the tent he was in and the tent pole fatally struck him on the head.

🔸 Bahram V, reigned from 421–438 C.E., and was the 14th king of the Sassanid Empire. He was often called Bahram-e Gur, (*gur* means onager). Bahram loved to hunt onagers, otherwise known as the Wild Asian Ass.

🔸 Khosrau II reigned from 590–628 C.E. and was the 22nd Sassanid king. His favorite horse was a black stallion called Shabdiz.

Scientific Revolution

● The Scientific Revolution took place over a period of time when new ideas in physics, astronomy, biology, human anatomy, chemistry, and other sciences arose. These contradicted prevailing ideas that had first been thought of in Ancient Greece and were adopted and held in Europe continually through the Middle Ages.

● Two centuries before English scientist Isaac Newton (1642–1726) said, "Objects at rest tend to remain at rest," Leonardo da Vinci, Italian scientist (1452–1519) said, "Nothing moves, unless it is moved upon."

● Though known for his work in cosmology, German Nicolaus Corpernicus (1473–1543) studied medicine and worked as a doctor.

● Italian scientist Galileo (1564–1642) believed the dark spots on the surface of the Moon were oceans. He named them "Maria" (for *mare*— ocean).

● In 1992 the Roman Catholic Church admitted wrongdoing on the part of the judges who convicted Galileo of heresy for endorsing Corpernicus' theory that the Earth revolved around the Sun. It did not, however, completely absolve Galileo for his part in the controversy, which led to him being held under house arrest for his "irreverent views" until his death in 1642.

● Johannes Kepler (1571–1630) a German scientist based his calculation of Jesus Christ's birth on data he collected watching a supernova in 1604.

S

Scotland

🐾 The official animal of Scotland is the unicorn. On the royal coat of arms, it appears chained because it was believed to be a wild animal. (Maybe someone should have been kind and let them know that unicorns never actually existed!)

🐾 The One O'Clock Gun in Edinburgh Castle fires every day at exactly 1 P.M. (except Sundays) in order to help ships' captains in the harbor to set their chronometers to the exact time.

🐾 That's no way to treat a lady! Mary, Queen of Scots (1542–1587) ascended to the Scottish throne when she was just one year old. Henry VIII of England (1491–1547) was keen to gain control over the country and so proposed a coupling with his five-year-old son Edward. And how did he do this? Not with flattery or gifts, but with war, which was later described by the writer Sir Walter Scott as the "rough wooing."

🐾 Robert the Bruce was king of Scotland from 1306–1329. He not only fought for Scottish independence (the Battle of Bannockburn in 1314 saw a significant defeat of the English) but is also thought to have died of leprosy. Recorded by historians as suffering from an "unclean disease," it is now thought that it was more likely syphilis, psoriasis, motor neuron disease, or maybe even a stroke that killed him.

🐾 In World War I, Scotland lost the greatest number of soldiers per head of population than any other century.

S

Seven Years' War, The

🐦 The Seven Years' War (1756–1763) is sometimes referred to as the "First World War" because it involved so many different countries and was global in its scale.

🐦 In Canada, France, and the United Kingdom, the Seven Years' War is also used to describe the North American portion of the conflict, though today the U.S. know it better as the French and Indian War (which started in 1754). Meanwhile in Quebec it is known as *La Guerre de la Conquête*, (The War of Conquest), while in India it is known as Third Carnatic War. The fighting between Prussia and Austria is called the Third Silesian War.

🐦 The failure of British Admiral John Byng to protect the island of Minorca from the French led to his execution, which French philosopher Voltaire later cited in his novel *Candide* (1759): "In this country, it is wise to kill an admiral from time to time to give courage to the others."

🐦 At the Battle of Warburg in North West Germany on July 31, 1760, the fighting was so fierce that the British hero Marquis of Granby lost his hat and wig but was still able to salute his commander-in-chief as he rode on by.

🐦 Granby was also regarded as a generous man because, knowing that after the war many soldiers had to fend for themselves, he set them up as innkeepers. This goes some way to explaining why so many pubs in England are called the Marquis of Granby.

S

Shakespeare's England

🐦 Under the powerful rule of Elizabeth I, England emerged as a leader of naval and commercial power in the Western world. This era was known as the Age of Shakespeare.

🐦 Key ingredients in deodorants in Elizabethan England included orris root, camomile, and alum.

🐦 Sex during breastfeeding was looked down on during this period of English history.

🐦 The Globe Theater in London (built in 1599) where Shakespeare's plays were performed also served as a brothel and gambling house.

🐦 Only men performed in Shakespeare's plays, with boys playing the female roles.

🐦 Sir Francis Drake became the most revered English sea captain of his generation at the time for his achievement of circumnavigating the world.

🐦 London was the heartbeat of England in Shakespeare's time and became a leading center of art and culture that was as vibrant then as it is today.

🐦 The population of the entire country was probably around three million. Today, it's nearly 60 million.

S

Sikhs

❧ The Sikhs are followers of Sikhism, a monotheistic religion founded in fifteenth-century Punjab, in India. Since its founding in the fifteenth century, Sikhism has become the world's fifth-largest religion and has some 26 million followers.

❧ It takes about 15 feet of cloth to wrap a Sikh turban around the head. It is not regarded as a hat.

❧ The Sikh holy book is called the *Guru Granth Sahib* and it is kept on a raised platform under a canopy. Sikhs will take off their shoes in the presence of the holy scriptures and will never turn their back on them. During festivals, the holy book is to be read continuously from start to finish, which takes about 48 hours.

❧ Banda Singh Bahadur (1670–1716) was a Sikh warrior and martyr who, upon his refusal to pledge allegiance to Islam, witnessed his four-year-old son being killed and then had pieces of flesh forced into his mouth. Then he himself was cut into pieces.

❧ Maharaja Ranjeet Singh, who ruled the sovereign country of Punjab from 1799 to 1839, was not only the founder of the Sikh Empire but he was known as a kind and fair ruler. He was much loved. Not only did he refuse to use capital punishment during his 40 year reign, but he would often mingle among the commoners in disguise to find out how they felt about his kingdom before implementing change.

Slave Castles

❧ Slave Castles were the stop-off point for slaves in Africa before they were herded onto ships and sent overseas. Elmina castle, a slave castle built by Portuguese traders in Ghana in 1482, is the oldest European structure built south of the equator and has recently been designated a UNESCO world heritage site.

❧ The Portuguese named the place they landed "Elmina" from the Portuguese word "mina," meaning a gold mine. They named the country, the "Gold Coast" because of the abundance of gold dust they found when they landed.

❧ It is believed that Christopher Columbus (1451–1506) even stopped over and visited Elmina before embarking on his trip to discover the New World.

❧ When the Portuguese first arrived in Ghana they had to conduct what was called the "Silent Trade." This was not because the trade was a secret. The language barrier made it difficult to barter, so traders used gestures and other means.

❧ Some ten million Africans were sold into slavery between the 1500s and 1800s by their own tribal elders in exchange for gunpowder, alcohol, and such novelties as mirrors.

S

Slavery

- Approximately 130,000 freed slaves became Union soldiers during the American Civil War (1861–65).

- Many slaves in America refused to eat as reprisal against the regime of slavery. Consequently, owners would force food down their throats or shovel hot molten lead on their heads in order to make them eat.

- Slave stealing was so common that steps were introduced to identity each slave to owner—often a branding with an iron on the slave's arm or on their chest.

- Known as "The Prophet" by his followers, Nat Turner and seven other slaves—killed the entire Hatchel family in August 1831. Turner soon began terrorizing other plantations in the area. Why? He interpreted a solar eclipse as a sign from God to act against the oppressors. He was executed in November of the same year.

- In 1831, William Lloyd Garrison, an American journalist began publishing the abolition newspaper called *The Liberator* in Boston. His most famous quote was: "I am in earnest, I will not equivocate, I will not excuse, I will not retreat a single inch, and I will be heard." He later founded the American Anti-Slavery Society in 1833.

- Harriet Tubman (circa 1820–1913) earned the moniker "Moses" for leading more than 300 slaves to freedom. Her reputation infuriated some slave owners who put up a $40,000 reward for her capture.

Song Dynasty

❧ Baidu.com, China's popular internet search engine, takes its name from a Song Dynasty (960–1279) poem, specifically the closing lines: "Restlessly I searched for her thousands, hundreds of ways./Suddenly I turned, and there she was in the receding light." Hundreds of ways is the literal meaning of *baidu* and interpreted as meaning a quest for perfection.

❧ Two ancient drains in China, remnants of the Song Dynasty, saved thousands of people in Ganzhou from severe flooding and landslides that destroyed neighboring areas in the summer of 2010. The drains were aptly named by their creator "Fortune" and "Longevity."

❧ Puppet theater was a popular form of entertainment during the Song Dynasty in China.

❧ At the time of the Song Dynasty, the biggest city in the world was Córdoba, Spain, with a population of approximately 450,000 people in the year 1000.

❧ Among the Song Dynasty social clubs that privileged city dwellers took part in were the Physical Fitness Club, Exotic Foods Club, West Lake Poetry Club, and Antique Collector's Club.

S

Space Exploration

꽃

• The explosion of Space Shuttle *Challenger* (1986) occurred just one minute 13 seconds after the flight began. The shuttle was 9 miles (14.5 km) above the Earth.

• There is a solar system called Upsilon Andromedae 44 light years from us, which is part of the constellation Andromeda.

• Mike Melvill, the pilot of the first private spacecraft—*SpaceShipOne*—was born in Johannesburg, South Africa.

• The Ancient Greeks named the Milky Way. They believed the points of light they saw were drops of milk from the goddess Hera.

S

• Ever wonder what microgravity will do to a sweet potato? Scientists did. In 2009 they sent some cuttings up in the Space Shuttle *Columbia*. The Center for Food and Environmental Systems for Human Exploration of Space published the results in the *Journal of American Society for Horticultural Science* where they explained that microgravity does not interfere with sweet potato root renewal.

• On November 3, 1957, Laika the Russian dog was the first animal in orbit. The dog survived the launch but probably not too much longer after that because her canister is suspected to have overheated. Suffice it to say, the dog had a *ruff* ride.

• When the *Apollo 11* lunar module, nicknamed the *Eagle*, landed on the Moon, it had only 30 seconds' worth of fuel to spare.

❧ When the astronauts from *Apollo 11* returned to Earth, they were quarantined for three weeks in case they brought dangerous space microbes with them.

❧ Not only have humans, dogs, and a monkey traveled to outer space, but also rats, ants, goldfish, jellyfish, worms, frogs, and sea urchins.

❧ In 1969, Astronaut John W. Young held a picture of Snoopy when the *Apollo 10* was about halfway to the Moon. Snoopy, who was not just an ace pilot, but also a superb astronaut, is the U.S. astronauts' mascot.

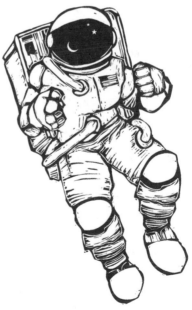

❧ Heavy duty ... A spacesuit weighs approximately 280 pounds (127 kg)—without the astronaut in it—and takes 45 minutes to put on.

❧ Each space shuttle astronaut is allocated 3.8 pounds (2 kg) of food every day.

❧ In April 2001, Dennis Tito paid $22 million to stay aboard the International Space Station for eight days and became the first space tourist ever.

Spanish Succession, War of

∼ The War of Spanish Succession (1701–1714) was essentially a struggle by several European powers to get their hands on the Spanish throne after the death of Charles II of Spain in 1700 in order to influence the balance of power in Europe.

∼ King Charles II was the only surviving son of the Hapsburg line. His father was King Philip IV of Spain and his mother was Mariana of Austria and Philip's own niece. So common was the custom of marrying uncle to niece that Empress Maria Anna of Austria was simultaneously Charles II's aunt and grandmother.

∼ Keep it in the family! In fact, *outbreeding* in Charles II's lineage appears to have ended in 1550, some 150 years before he was born.

∼ Perhaps as a result, Charles II is sometimes referred to as *El Hechizado* ("The Hexed") given the numerous physical and mental disabilities he suffered from. Charles himself preferred to believe that they were the result of witchcraft.

S

Sports

❧ Hot wheels! When they couldn't be out riding the surf, 1950s, boys (and girls) in California put wheels on their boards, and skateboarding was born. At first it was called, not surprisingly, "sidewalk surfing."

❧ Eskimos have some unique sports. One of them involves attaching a 16-pound (7.25-kg) weight to your ear. The player to walk the longest distance holding the weight wins.

❧ The Olympic Games were not held in 1916, 1940, or 1944 because of World War I and World War II.

❧ A badminton shuttle can travel in excess of 180 mph (290 km/h). Get into the wing of things—high-quality shuttles are also made from the feathers from the left wing of a goose.

S

❧ Basketball is one of American's favorite sports. Unbeknown to many, the slam-dunk was made illegal in 1967, and was only made legal again nine years later.

❧ A Nascar driver can shed 5–10 pounds (2–4.5 kg) in sweat during a race.

❧ Prior to the 1930 American League season and the 1931 National League season, baseballs that bounced over or through the outfield fence were considered to be home runs.

Stalin, Joseph

◆ As a child Stalin (1878–1953) suffered from smallpox, which left him with a permanent mark on his face and unable to bend his left arm fully at the elbow. His left arm was therefore several inches shorter than his right.

◆ When he was young, Stalin had actually trained to be a priest but was kicked out of the seminary for "revolutionary activities."

◆ By 1902, Stalin had assumed the underground name Koba, after a fictitious Georgian hero who was similar to Robin Hood.

◆ Born as Iosif Vissarionovich Dzhugashvili, he chose the new name of Stalin, which means "man of steel." He was also known as "Father of Nations," "Brilliant Genius of Humanity," "Great Architect of Communism," and "Gardener of Human Happiness."

◆ Stalin is rumored to have met Hitler on only one occasion—and that was in a train carriage in 1939.

◆ Stalin died of a cerebral hemorrhage in March 1953, but not before suffering a long period of mental deterioration in which he experienced delusions of persecution by others.

Stone Age

❧ The Stone Age has a vague time span but is generally regarded as the point in human evolution at which humans began to use stone tools, some 2.5 million years ago. Often, the Stone Age is subdivided into the Paleolithic, Mesolithic, and Neolithic periods.

❧ What's for dinner? Given that food at that time was of rather large proportions (elephants, horses, bison) early Stone Agers came up with an ingenious method for hunting. They would stampede the animals off of cliffs and into swamps and then butcher them. In America they only needed to do this once a year, and that gave them enough food for the whole winter.

❧ People of the Stone Age were also quite artistic, decorating the walls of their caves with paintings. In order to make the paints, they would mix different colored minerals with blood.

❧ Paging Dr. House! Stone Age humans were also adept at medicine and had some novel ways of dealing with a headache. With their tools, they learned how to peel back the scalp and drill holes into the skull with flint—presumably to relieve pressure or repair a head wound.

❧ In Australia it seemed to be the custom among Stone Age men to have their front row of teeth knocked out as a sign of their manhood.

❧ One archeologist by the name of David Cahen, spent months studying an archeological site in Belgium. His findings were so detailed he was even able to deduce that one of the Stone Age toolmakers had been left-handed!

S

Stonewall Rebellion

S

- The Stonewall Rebellion was a series of riots by gay activists that began in the early hours of June 28, 1969. It took place outside a bar called the Stonewall Inn in New York City. Many consider this event to have launched the gay rights movement.

- The police had targeted the Stonewall Inn because of its illegal sale of alcohol, and announced that employees would be arrested and lined up against a wall to check their ID. A passive situation quickly turned aggressive when the police violently attempted to load someone into a waiting van and the crowd began hurling stones and bottles.

- *The Daily News* ran an article about the uprising entitled, "Homo Nest Raided, Queen Bees are Stinging Mad."

- The funeral for movie star and chanteuse Judy Garland, a huge gay icon, took place the day before the riot.

- After the riot, the sale of gay publications spiked. Among them: *Gay Flames* (New York), *Lavender Vision* (Boston), and *Killer Dyke* (Chicago).

- In 1969, New York City allowed bars to refuse service to lesbians, gay men, bisexuals, and transvestites.

Stowe, Harriet Beecher

- Harriet Beecher Stowe (1811–1896) wrote many books that addressed the issues of racism and slavery in America. Her most famous title was *Uncle Tom's Cabin* (1852). She gained very little profit from their publication due to the number of unauthorized copies published outside of the U.S. and the pricing structure of the publishing industry at that time.

- Stowe became so popular overseas that a petition signed by half a million English, Scottish, and Irish women and addressed to the women of the United States finally led to Stowe making a trip to Europe in 1853.

- Stowe was fortunate enough to return to Europe again in 1856 where she met not only Queen Victoria, but Charles Dickens, Elizabeth Barrett Browning, and George Eliot.

- In 1862 Stowe met Abraham Lincoln for the first time. It is claimed he said, "So you are the little woman who wrote the book that started this great war!"—a rather trite description of the book *Uncle Tom's Cabin*, which depicted the cruelty of slavery.

- *Uncle Tom's Cabin* is set—in part—in Sandusky, Ohio.

- Stowe managed to publish a book a year between 1862 and 1884.

S

Suffragettes

꧁ ❦ ꧂

❧ The suffrage movement was a campaign that petitioned for women's right to vote and run for office. The first place in the U.S. that allowed women unrestricted suffrage was the Wyoming Territory in 1869, followed by the appointment of its first female justice of the peace Esther Morris, one year later.

❧ The Suffragettes was the name given to the members of the British Women's Social and Political Union founded in 1903 to campaign for the right of women to vote.

❧ To draw attention and support to their cause, they interrupted political meetings, chained themselves to railings, broke windows, attempted arson, slashed pictures, and destroyed property. One lady named Emily Davidson threw herself in front of the king of England's horse, and died from the injuries she sustained.

❧ Lucy Burns (1879–1966) was a prominent and militant suffragist who fought the cause in both the U.S. and Great Britain and spent more time in prison than any other suffragist.

❧ Meanwhile Emmeline Pankhurst (1858–1928) was one of the most famous suffragettes in Great Britain. She was jailed at least ten times and subjected to brutality in prison.

S

✒ As a means of putting pressure on the government, many women in Great Britain stopped paying tax and adopted the slogan "No Vote, No Tax." So the Government simply seized items owned by the people who refused to pay their taxes and auctioned them off to the highest bidder.

✒ Here kitty, kitty! Because the suffragettes in Great Britain often resorted to hunger strikes while in prison to make their point, parliament passed an act to have the starving women released and then re-arrested once they had recovered. This became commonly known as the Cat and Mouse Act.

✒ In 1872, Susan B. Anthony, a prominent civil rights leader, was arrested along with three of her sisters for illegally voting in the re-election of Ulysses S. Grant in Rochester, New York. At her trial the judge ordered the jury to find her guilty without discussion and issued her with a fine. Wanting the trial to go to appeal, Susan refused to pay, but the judge refused to arrest her, thus denying her the possibility of appeal.

Sumerians and Sumer Civilization

⚬❦ Sumer love … Sumer is the earliest known civilization that spanned some 3,000 years and which existed in what is modern day Iraq. It is from the Sumerian city of Uruk that modern day Iraq gets its name.

⚬❦ Because it was the birthplace of writing, the wheel, agriculture, the arch, and irrigation, Sumer is also known as the Cradle of Civilization.

⚬❦ The Sumerians were known to refer to themselves as "the black-headed people".

S ⚬❦ Gilgamesh was the fifth king of Uruk and ruled around 5700 B.C.E. The *Epic of Gilgamesh* is an ancient poem and is regarded as the first work of literature in which Gilgamesh is described as two parts god and one part man.

⚬❦ In the *Epic of Gilgamesh*, the name of the 180-pound (82-kg) axe he carried was called the Might of Heroes.

⚬❦ A man called Endiku is credited with being the world's first sidekick as he and Gilgamesh embarked on multiple adventures in the *Epic of Gilgamesh*.

⚬❦ Sargon the Great ruled during the Akkadian period (twenty-third and twenty-second centuries B.C.E.) and it is said that he was the son of a high priestess who put her son in a basket and sent him down river.

Sung Dynasty

- The dynasty was divided into two eras: the Northern Sung (960–1127 C.E.) and Southern Sung (1127–1279 C.E.).

- New technologies, including gunpowder, were developed during the Sung Dynasty. It was first used for fireworks and eventually in weaponry to create the first missiles, which were made of bamboo poles stuffed with gunpowder.

- *Nanhai One*, a Chinese merchant ship from the Sung Dynasty, was discovered in 1987 off the southern coast of China. An estimated 60,000 to 80,000 relics were on this ship including porcelain coins, gold, and silver.

- The practice of binding the feet of female children, and emperors taking concubines were born out of this dynasty.

- The Sung Dynasty had 18 emperors and lasted for 320 years.

- Advances were made in medicine at the time. The first autopsy was performed in China during the Sung Dynasty in about 1145 C.E.

S

Tet Offensive

The Tet Offensive was a military campaign during the Vietnam War (1955–1975). On January 31, 1968, on the first celebrated day of the Lunar New Year—also known as the festival of Tet—the Vietnamese Communists launched a major offensive throughout South Vietnam.

The communist forces had attacked about 90 towns and hundreds of villages in spite of the presence of 500,000 U.S. troops.

According to U.S. figures, 4,959 Vietcong had been killed and 1,862 captured while 232 American and 300 South Vietnamese troops had been killed with 929 and 747 wounded.

The Vietnamese call the Vietnam War *Chien Tranh Chong My Curu Nuoc*, or "The War against the Americans to save the nation."

The rebels captured the former Vietnamese imperial capital, Hue, which took several days to recover. By then, the North Vietnamese had massacred 3,000 civilians.

Two-thirds of the American men who served in Vietnam were volunteers and 70 percent were killed during the war.

A noodle cafe in Ho Chi Minh City served as home base for the F100 Viet Cong cell, which took part in the offensive. It's still there, but is now serving "peace noodles."

◆ Ironically, radio broadcasters in both North and South Vietnam had told listeners a ceasefire would take place for two days during the holiday. Instead one of the bloodiest battles of the war was launched, claiming thousands of lives and turning the tide of war against the anticommunist allies.

◆ Most historians agree the Tet Offensive was a massive defeat for the communists even though it is remembered as the turning point for America losing the war.

Thirteen Colonies, The

❧ The Thirteen Colonies were originally British colonies on the Atlantic coast of North America, which eventually declared independence during the American Revolution. North Carolina was home to the Roanoke Colony and on August 18, 1587, was the birthplace of Virginia Dare, the first child born in America to English parents.

❧ The Big Tulip? New York was once part of New Netherlands, with the lower tip of Manhattan being called New Amsterdam. Only when England's King Charles II seized the area from the Dutch in the 1660s did he decide on the name New York, after his brother, the Duke of York.

❧ The thirteenth colony to be established in 1732 was Georgia, which was specifically set up to offload Britain's debtors. The British government was concerned by the number of debt prisoners in England, so the colony was built to give the "worthy poor" a second chance.

❧ Delaware was the first of the thirteen original states to ratify the Constitution of the United States. Delaware's Blue Hen Army is so-called because during the Revolutionary War, Captain John Caldwell was a fan and owner of blue fighting roosters.

❧ Proud Mary—Maryland got its name from King Charles II wife, Queen Henrietta Maria (aka Queen Mary).

❧ Connecticut was the the fifth colony to became a state in 1788, but it is home to the oldest U.S. newspaper still in print—*The Hartford Courant*—which was established in 1764.

🐦 Named after King George I of England (1660–1727), the official state fish of Georgia is the largemouth bass.

🐦 In Massachusetts (and Maine, which was once part of Massachusetts, until 1820) the third Monday in April is a legal holiday called Patriot's Day.

🐦 Rhode Island was the first colony to declare independence from England (1776) but the last colony to become a state. It was also the smallest colony and is still the smallest state, though not actually an island!

Thirty Years' War

❧ The Thirty Years War (1618–1648) was the result of several decades of simmering tension between the Protestants and Catholics throughout central Europe, which finally erupted into open conflict involving most European states. It was in fact four successive wars. Such damage was done to central Europe that it took more than 150 years for the area to recover.

❧ Keep away from the windows! The Thirty Years' War was sparked off when discontented Protestant Bohemians stormed Prague Castle in 1618 and threw two of the Catholic Imperial ministers (Wilhelm Graf Slavata and Jaroslav Borzita Graf von Martinicz) out of the window and into a moat filled with manure. This act gave us the word "defenestration," (from the latin "tenestrun" meaning window), which, according to the *Britannica World Language Dictionary*, means: "the act of throwing out of a window … used specifically as popular vengeance in Bohemia (now the Czech Republic)."

❧ Albrecht von Wallenstein was a Bohemian nobleman who backed the Catholic cause in the Thirty Years' War and relied heavily on horoscopes, particularly from Johannes Kepler, a key figure in the seventeenth century scientific revolution.

❧ The Thirty Years' War was devastating in its impact as soldiers raped, pillaged, and murdered their way across central Europe, sometimes wiping whole villages off the map. It took a particular toll of the population of the German states. Estimates state that between 15–30 percent of the population in these areas died during the conflict, with the region of Württemberg losing three-quarters of its population!

❧ The Swedish King Gustavus Adolphus backed the Protestants. He decided to enter the fray in 1630 with the first army built up from universal conscription, wearing the first army uniforms, carrying the first light artillery to give them maneuverability on the battlefield, and receiving regular pay. Needless to say they were highly incentivized in their aims to crush the Catholics.

❧ Not only did poor King Gustavus end up dying on the battlefield in a cavalry charge after having been shot three times, his body was then plundered and his royal ring stolen.

❧ At the end of the war—more a result of exhaustion than victory—the Peace of Westphalia left the Holy Roman Empire divided into more than 300 separate German sovereignties, some covering no more than a few square miles.

Trademarks and Patents

> It was during the Middle Ages (fifth to fifteenth century) that craftsmen began using marks to indicate who had made which specific item. Bellmakers were among the first to make this a regular habit.

> The Bakers Marking Law, passed in England in 1266, is one of the earliest known records of officially legislating trademarks. It details how stamps or pinpricks should be used on bread.

> The first ever U.S. Patent was U.S Patent No. 1X: "Method of producing pot ash and pearl ash," which were fertilizers. It was issued to Samuel Hopkins on July 31, 1790.

> The first recorded U.S. Patent issued to a woman was issued to Mary Kies on May 5, 1809. It was U.S. Patent No. 1041X for "Weaving Straw with Silk or Thread". Other women probably recorded patents before Kies, but it is likely they would have done so under their husband's name.

> The first African-American to get a patent went by the name of Thomas Jennings and his patent was for "Dry Scouring of Clothes" (U.S. Patent No. 3306X—March 3, 1821).

Not exactly the Pony Express! The patent office pony was a key tool in the early days of the Patent Office. Messengers rode the pony over to the State Department to receive the signatures of the Secretary of State, the Attorney General, and the President on issuing patents. In June 1827, the Patent Office pony was stolen, but was eventually recovered three months later. The phrase "riding the Patent Office pony" became a metaphor for working at the Patent Office.

Up until 1880, the U.S. Patent and Trademark Office required models of the inventions to be supplied when possible.

Many of the products that we use every day once had their own trademark, including aspirin, cellophane, nylon, thermos, and escalator. These were once all brand named and trademarked products.

Transcendentalists

- Transcendentalism was the name given to a group of new ideas in literature, religion, culture, and philosophy that emerged in New England in the early to the mid-nineteenth century. It began as a protest against the general state of culture and society.

- The movement was led by American Ralph Waldo Emerson (1803–1882), who was an essayist, philosopher, and poet, and had even worked for a time as a Unitarian minister.

- *The Dial,* a transcendentalist magazine, was first published in 1840. It was edited by the American Rights activist and feminist Margaret Fuller.

- Almost all transcendentalists had been schoolteachers at some point in their lives.

- A canoe trip in 1839 prompted Henry David Thoreau (1817–1862) to steer away from being a schoolteacher and become a poet.

- After the funeral of Henry Wadsworth Longfellow (1807–1882), Ralph Waldo Emerson, who had been Longfellow's friend for four decades, confessed to forgetting the name of the deceased, but added, "he had a beautiful soul."

- Henry David Thoreau was born David Henry Thoreau.

American novelist Nathaniel Hawthorne (1804–1864) was on a trip in New Hampshire's White Mountains with Franklin Pierce (an American politician and lawyer) when he died.

Louisa May Alcott (1832–1888), author of the children's classic *Little Women*, was the daughter of lesser-known transcendentalist Bronson Alcott. In one of Louisa May Alcott's early works—*Perilous Play*—the leading characters meet at a hashish party.

Henry David Thoreau was sent to search for Margaret Fuller's manuscript on the revolution in Italy (1848), which was lost when she and her husband and son died in a ship that went down off the coast of Long Island in 1850.

Transportation

T

✤ Fixed wheels on carts were invented in 3500 B.C.E. Though we don't know who invented it first, the oldest wheel was discovered in Mesopotamia.

✤ The Egyptians invented the sailing boat around 3100 B.C.E. The boats were made of papyrus reeds bundled together and had a sheet of papyrus for the sail. At this time, the sail could be only used when sailing in one direction. When traveling against the wind the boat had to be rowed.

✤ The Chinese had invented the compass hundreds of years before the Europeans learned to use it in the twelfth century.

✤ Hot air balloons were used for observation platforms in World War I.

✤ In 1863, the first subway was built in London, England.

✤ In 1640 public transportation in England was divided into social classes. The upper class traveled in the carriages while the poor had to stand on the roof, above the luggage, and face the risk of falling.

✤ In 1913, the Panama Railroad transported 2,916,657 passengers across the Isthmus. The railroad suffered the most congested per-mile traffic of any railroad in the world.

✤ Charles Lindbergh took four sandwiches on board his celebrated 1927 first solo transatlantic flight ever. He took off in the "Spirit of St. Lewis" from New York and landed in Le Bourget Field outside Paris thirty-three and a half hours later. A crowd of 100,000 greeted his arrival.

➤ The first hybrid car available to the public in the U.S. was the Honda Insight, which sold for $18,880 in 1999.

➤ It cost approximately $400 million to build the Panama Canal.

➤ When Chuck Yeager—the renowned World War II and Vietnam War pilot who was the first person to break the sound barrier in flight—was four years old his baby sister was killed by his older brother in a shotgun accident.

➤ In 1903, England was the first country to set a national speed limit. It was a terrifying 20 miles per hour (32 km/h).

➤ John Dunlop was the Scottish veterinarian who perfected and patented the design of a pneumatic (air-filled) tire. (He first used an inflated garden hose.) Dunlop was motivated by the desire to relieve his son of headaches he got from riding his tricycle. Until Dunlop's invention, the tires were hard and the rides bumpy.

Treaty of Versailles, The

- The treaty itself was signed on June 28, 1919, exactly five years to the day after Archduke Franz Ferdinand was assassinated by a Serbian terrorist group, the catalyst for World War I to begin.

- Article 231 of the treaty was better known as the "War Guilt Clause." In this clause Germany is forced to accept full responsibility for the war reparations, including making payments to the Entente powers of France, Great Britain, and Russia.

- Had Germany paid the total cost of the reparations for World War I, as stated in the Treaty of Versailles—132 billion marks or $31.4 billion—it would have taken them until 1988 to pay it off.

- The Heavenly Twins was the nickname given to two British delegates—Judge Lord Sumner and banker Lord Cunliffe—who were responsible for ironing out the terms of the treaty imposed on Germany. Three reasons are given for this nickname: first, the "astronomical" sums they were seeking to extract from Germany; second, the beatific smiles they adopted when rendering a judgment; and third, they were inseparable for the duration of the time they worked out the treaty.

- Aspirin and Heroin both lost their status as registered trademarks in Russia, France, the UK, and the U.S. as part of the war reparations of the Treaty of Versailles. This is why we no longer need to capitalize these words when writing them.

T

⌖ Article 246 of the Treaty stated that within six months of coming into effect, the skull of the Sultan Mkwawa had to be handed over to His Britannic Majesty's Government. The skull was significant in that it belonged to a tribal chief in German East Africa who had opposed the occupation. Following a protracted battle, rather than submit to the Germans, Sultan Mkwawa shot himself in the head. The Germans then took his skull to Berlin. After the Treaty of Versailles the British wanted to return the skull to Tanganyika as thanks to the Wahehe tribe's cooperation during the war and as proof that German power had been quashed.

⌖ Article 227 of the Treaty charged the former German Emperor Wilhelm II (1859–1941) with supreme offences against international morality and he was to be tried as a war criminal.

Trung Sisters

❧ The Trung Sisters—Trung Trac and Trung Nhi—were two Vietnamese women who, between 40–43 C.E., liberated Vietnam from 247 years of Chinese domination. They rallied their troops through acts of bravery, such as killing a tiger and then using its skin to write a proclamation for people to follow them and rise up against their oppressors.

❧ Trung Trac, the eldest sister, is recorded as having a "brave and fearless disposition."

❧ The army, which was built by the Trung sisters to defeat the Chinese was made up of 80,000 people and included 36 women, one of whom was their mother.

T

❧ Phung Thi Chinh was a noble woman and a captain to a group of the Trung sisters' soldiers. She went into battle heavily pregnant and is said to have given birth on the front line, then scooped up her child in one arm and continued the fight with her sword in the other.

❧ After their victory, Trung Trac was proclaimed by the people to become their ruler and renamed "She-king Trung."

❧ The Chinese fought back, of course, and legend has it that one tactic they used was to fight naked so as to shame the women who were going into battle.

When the Trung sisters were eventually defeated in 43 C.E. they felt they had no other option but to commit suicide in the Hat River (the Hat Giang).

To this day, Vietnamese soldiers are said to carry pictures of the Trung sisters as a source of inspiration and courage.

Turks and Turkey

☙ The Turks are an ethnic group native to Turkey but which also exist in sizable minorities across Europe, Asia, and Africa. The capital of Turkey, Istanbul, which is one of the oldest cities in the world, is actually built on two continents, straddling the Bosphorus Strait, keeping one foot in Europe and the other in Asia.

☙ When the Republic of Turkey was formed in 1923 following on from the Ottoman Empire, the first party to be established was the People Party of Women (Kadinlar Halk Firkasi) founded by Nezihe Muhiddin (1889–1958). But because the party was founded by women it was not recognized by the Turkish state.

☙ The wearing of a fez—a red, brimless hat with a tassel—was legally banned in Turkey in 1925 as a means of modernizing the country and moving away from what was regarded as "oriental" cultural identity.

☙ It didn't start with Starbucks! It was the Turks who first introduced coffee to Europe.

☙ Turquoise, the precious stone and the color associated with it, gets its name from Turkey because that is where it traveled through on its way to the West

☙ One of the oldest-known shipwrecks in the world is a fourteenth-century B.C.E. Late Bronze Age find, known as the Uluburun shipwreck. It was found off the south coast of Turkey near Kas.

✺ A little far from the North Pole? St. Nicholas (270–346), who was the precursor to Santa Clause, was actually born in Patara, which can be found on Turkey's Mediterranean Coast.

✺ The sport of camel wrestling, where two male camels battle it out after having been taunted by a female camel in heat, is most common in Turkey. There, camels are specifically bred for the competition.

Umar ibn al-Khattab

❧ Born in Mecca and also known as Omar the Great or Farooq the Great (circa 586–644 C.E.), he was one of the most powerful and influential Muslim rulers. Unusual for that time, Umar not only learned to read and write from a young age, but he also became proficient at martial arts, horseback riding, and wrestling.

❧ Friends in high places! Umar was good friends with the prophet Mohammed—so much so that in 625 Umar let his daughter Hafsah marry him!

❧ For the first time in 500 years, it was Umar who let the Jews practice their religion openly in the Holy Land and live in Jerusalem.

U

❧ Umar made a point of paying his staff and governors high salaries because he believed this would lessen the chances of corruption.

❧ After the Battle of Yamamah, the war that established the supremacy of Islam in Central Arabia, hundreds of memorizers of the Qur'an were killed and it was Umar who persuaded Abu Bakr—the prophet Mohammed's father-in-law—to put together the Qur'an in book form.

❧ Like many other leaders, Umar was fond of getting down with the locals and touring the city of Medina at night to check up on how his rule was working with the people.

United Arab Emirates

❧ The UAE is a federation of seven states—or emirates—located in the southeastern Arabian Peninsula. They include Abu Dhabi, Dubai, Sharjah, Ajman, Umm al-Quwain, Ras al-Khaimah, and Fujairah. Before 1971, the UAE was known as the Trucial States because of the nineteenth-century truce brokered between the United Kingdom and the seven Arab sheikhs.

❧ Between the eighteenth and early twentieth centuries the emirates were also known as the "Pirate Coast" because the British shipping industry was continually being harassed by pirates up and down the coast.

❧ In Dubai there are no taxes on income and no personal taxes. This may go a long way to explaining why 80 percent of Dubai's residents are foreigners.

❧ Chain, chain, chain ... In 1999, Dubai goldsmiths made the world's longest gold chain. It measured 2.6 miles (4.2 km) in length and weighed more than 440 pounds (200 kg). After its unveiling, the chain was cut into smaller pieces and sold to be worn as necklaces and bracelets.

❧ In the eye of the beholder ... The UAE has recently hosted one of the most unusual competitions ever—a beauty pageant for camels. In April 2008, Abu Dhabi hosted its second Camel Beauty Contest with prizes worth as much as $9 million as a tribute to the animals that are central to Arab culture.

U

United Nations, The

◆ The United Nations was established in 1945 following the failure of the League of Nations (1919–1946)—an international body which the United States never joined. Whether or not the League of Nations could have succeeded, ensuring that war never broke out again is one of the great "what ifs" of modern history.

◆ One of the earliest critics of the UN was the French President Charles de Gaulle (1890–1970) who referred to it as *le machin* ("the thingy") because he did not think it could maintain world peace.

◆ Hindustani may be the third most popular language in the world, but it is still not one of the official languages of the UN. The six official languages are, in fact, Arabic, Chinese, English, French, Russian, and Spanish.

◆ The land on which the United Nation headquarters sits in New York City is considered international territory. This means the UN building itself does not have to meet New York City's fire safety or building codes.

◆ The only one nonmember observer state in the UN is the Holy See in Vatican City.

◆ The United Nations is funded by its member states and the U.S., which pays the largest sum, is consistently late with its payments. But the U.S. is not alone because, apparently, only 40 of the 192 member states actually pay on time.

Uruguay

 Uruguay is the second-smallest country in South America (after Suriname) and is slightly smaller than the state of Washington. The official name for the country is actually the Oriental Republic of Uruguay. The name "Uruguay" means "river where the painted birds live."

 In the nineteenth century, Uruguayans divided themselves along two political lines: the liberal Colorados (reds) and the conservative Blancos (whites). They could be identified by the color of their armbands. The Colorados had originally started out with blue armbands, but switched to red when they found that the blue ones faded in the sun.

 From 1839 to 1852, Uruguayans were engaged in a civil war known as the "Guerra Grande," which translates as Big War.

 Giusseppe Garibaldi (1807–1882), an Italian political and military figure (dubbed the "Hero of Two Worlds" for his military leadership in both Europe and South America), was working as a math teacher in the capital Montevideo when war broke out. He eventually led the Italian Legion in the besieged city, and was later made head of the Uruguayan navy.

 In the early 1960s, a small group of urban guerrillas was formed. Called the Tupamaros, they would rob stores and banks and redistribute the lot among the poor—a modern-day bunch of Robin Hoods.

U

U.S. Constitution, The

The U.S. Constitution has 4,440 words and not only is it one of the oldest surviving constitutions, but it is also the shortest written constitution of any government in the world.

One of the more obvious misspellings in the U.S. Constitution is the word "Pennsylvania," which is wrongly spelled "Pensylvania" above the names of the signatories.

U For all that it is meant to represent, the word "democracy" does not appear once in the Constitution.

The oldest person to sign the Constitution was Benjamin Franklin (1706–1790) at 81 years of age. The youngest was Jonathan Dayton (1760–1824) of New Jersey, who was 26 years old.

James Madison (1751–1836) was the first to arrive in Philadelphia for the Constitutional Convention. He arrived in February, three months before the convention began, bearing the blueprint for the new Constitution.

◦❧ Thomas Jefferson (1743–1826) did not sign the Constitution because he was serving as U.S. minister to France during the Convention. Meanwhile John Adams (1735–1826) was serving as the U.S. minister to Great Britain, so he couldn't show up either.

◦❧ The Constitution does not set forth requirements for the right to vote. Hence at the outset of the Union, only male property-owners could vote and women were excluded. African-Americans were not considered citizens. Native American People were not given the right to vote until 1924.

◦❧ There was initially a question as to how to address the President. The Senate proposed that he be addressed as "His Highness the President of the United States of America and Protector of their Liberties." Both the House of Representatives and the Senate compromised and the term agreed upon was "President of the United States."

◦❧ The first ten amendments, known as the Bill of Rights, were added in 1791 to prevent the federal government from becoming too powerful, and to protect the individual rights of all Americans.

◦❧ The U.S. Constitution is also known as the "Bundle of Compromises."

◦❧ Party poopers? Only 12 of the 13 original states actually took part in writing the U.S. Constitution. Rhode Island did not attend the Constitutional Convention.

USSR—Union of Soviet Socialist Republics

 The Soviet Union (1922–1991) was the amalgamation of 15 Eurasian and Baltic republics (Armenia, Azerbaijan, Belarus, Estonia, Georgia, Kazakstan, Kyrgyzstan, Latvia, Lithuania, Moldova, Russia, Tajikistan, Turkmenistan, Ukraine, Uzbekistan) under a single-party political system, led from Moscow. The USSR went on to become one of the world's two main superpowers in opposition to the United States during the Cold War.

 The Great Purge (1936–38) was the name given to a series of campaigns that saw the Soviet Union suppress and remove any persons who were thought to be critical of or opposed to the fledgling regime. At its peak in 1937–38, the NKVD (secret police) arrested more than 1.5 million people and shot 681,692—making it an average of 1,000 executions a day.

 Order 270, issued by Stalin in July 1941, ordered that any Soviet soldiers who allowed themselves to be captured by the Germans during World War II would be declared an enemy of the state. Stalin's own son would become a victim of this order. Stalin refused to accept a prisoner exchange with the Germans, so his son died as a prisoner of war in 1943.

🐦 The Siege of Leningrad lasted from September of 1941 to January of 1944 during World War II. It became the longest known siege of a city since Biblical times, lasting some 900 days.

🐦 Despite the differences in economic and socio-political principles between the Soviet Union and the U.S., the Amtorg Trading Corporation was established by Armand Hammer (affiliated with, but not named after, Arm & Hammer) in 1924. It acted as the Soviet representative in the U.S. for Soviet firms that still wanted to conduct foreign trade.

🐦 SMERSH was the Army of the Soviet Union's counter-intelligence department. It was founded in the 1940s to neutralize anti-Soviet conspirators. The name is phonetically similar to the Russian words for death and tornado and was made even more famous by Ian Fleming (1908–1964), British author of the James Bond series. In his books, he portrayed SMERSH as an organization looking to subvert the West.

🐦 On February 9, 1961, Leonid Brezhnev (1906–1982) General Secretary of the Communist Party of the Soviet Union (1964–1982) was on a plane flying to the Republic of Guinea, which came under attack by French fighters. The pilot managed to evade the attack.

Venice

- The Arsenal, founded in 1104 in Venice, was the world's first factory. The shipyard produced one warship nearly every day.

- Giacomo Casanova, the infamous womanizer was born in 1725 in Venice.

- Teatro La Fenice was founded in 1790 and destroyed by fire in 1996. Giuseppe Verdi's (1813–1901) operas *Rigoletto*, *La Traviata*, and *Simon Boccanegra* were all premiered there.

- During World War II, Venice was not bombed but was seriously damaged by a flood. Water levels reached 6 feet 6 inches (2 m) higher than usual. Today, signs marking the height of the water during the flood are still visible.

- Venice is the only European city with public transportation that relies entirely on water.

- There was once a Russian Embassy in the Villa Maravege, now called Pensione Accademia, along the Grand Canal.

- In 1582, the Venetian government hosted an unusual contest to find an artist who would paint the biggest painting in the world.

- In the 1300s and 1400s, the maximum number of days a Jewish person could stay in Venice was 15.

Vietnam War

🐦 As in the Korean War, U.S. Congress never actually declared war against Vietnam. This is why it is often commonly known as the Vietnam conflict.

🐦 The average age of a U.S. soldier in the Vietnam conflict was 22 and the average age of those killed was 23. Out of the some 58,100 soldiers killed in Vietnam, five were only 16 years old and the oldest was 62.

🐦 The first U.S. victim of the Vietnam war could be said to be Lt. Col. A. Peter Dewey who was shot on September 26, 1945, after having been mistaken for a Frenchman. But as the conflict between the U.S. and Vietnam was not fully underway at the time, some sources cite Major Dale R. Buis and Master Sergent Chester M. Ovnand to be the first victims when they were killed at Bienhoa in 1959.

🐦 The most successful Vietnam vet to date is Frederick W. Smith, who founded and became CEO of Federal Express. Smith did two tours of duty between 1966 and 1969

🐦 Meanwhile Al Gore went to Vietnam from 1969 to 1971, even though he objected to the conflict and went on to attain the highest political office for a Vietnam vet: Vice President of the United States of America.

🐦 Agent Orange was not the only herbicide/defoliant used in the Vietnam conflict. The U.S. Military also sprayed Agent Blue, Green, White, Purple, and Pink. But it was Agent Orange that contained dioxin, which was later linked to a wide variety of heath problems and birth defects.

V

Vikings

🐦 Vikings were big on personal grooming and hygiene. Not only have excavations from the Viking Age unearthed tweezers, razors, and combs, but they were also known to bathe once a week and, in Scandinavian languages, Saturday is referred to as "washing day."

🐦 Vikings also had an impact on our calendar because the days of the week are remnants of a combination of Roman and Viking culture:

Monday = "mood day"
Tuesday = "Tyr's day" (Norse god of heroic glory)
Wednesday = "Wodin's day" (Anglo spelling of Odin, a great Norse god)
Thursday = "Thor's day"
Friday = "Freyja's day"
Saturday = Roman god Saturn
Sunday = "Sun's day"

🐦 The Berserkers were a tribe of Norsemen who took their name from the Old Norse word "bare-sark," which means "bare of shirt." They were in the habit of going unarmored into battle—hence the word "berserk."

🐦 Barking mad! After having conquered the tribes of the Danish peninsula, the Swedish Vikings installed a dog by the name of Rekkae to be their king. But the joke did not end there. When Rekkae eventually shuffled off to meet his maker, the Swedes then installed a poodle by the name of King Snio to take the lead. Alas Snio did not meet with a happy end. He was eaten alive by lice.

❧ During the eighth century the Vikings were known to make the strongest swords of their day, and did so with the help of ducks. By feeding ducks iron shavings, the ducks produced (possibly as a result of digestion) carbon-laced feces. These were gathered, hammered, and made into steel rods. The rods were then twisted with iron and hammered again into swords, which proved their metal on the battlefield.

❧ The first portable barbecue? The Vikings came up with an ingenious way to start a fire. First the Vikings harvested the touchwood fungus from oak and beech trees. They pounded the fungus flat, charred it in a fire, and then boiled it in urine for up to two days. The result was a portable piece of touchwood infused with sodium nitrate (from the urine). It would smoulder slowly but not burn. And you could carry it around, too!

Wales

~ Wales is a country in the western part of British Isles and is part of the United Kingdom, yet it is not represented on the Union Jack flag.

~ One of the longest place names that can be found is a village in Wales, named: Llanhyfryddawelllehynafolybarcudprindanfygythiadtrienusyrhafnauole. This means "a quiet beautiful village, an historic place with rare kite under threat from wretched blades."

~ The patron saint of Wales is St. David who actually came from Wales (as opposed to St. George, patron saint of England and St. Andrew, patron saint of Scotland, who both came from somewhere else).

~ Dude looks like a lady! The Rebecca Riots (1839–1843) were a series of protests that took place in Wales. The rioters—usually men dressed as women—protested against the unfair taxation caused by the tollgates. The rioters were named after a woman in the Bible named Rebecca because, in the Book of Genesis, chapter 22, verse 60 it says, "And they blessed Rebekah and said unto her, Thou art our sister, be thou the mother of thousands of millions, and let thy seed *possess the gate* of those which hate them."

~ Welshmen were responsible for a great many achievements including: the mapping of Canada (David Thompson); the invention of lawn tennis (Major Walter Clopton Wingfield); the founding of the *New York Times* (George Jones); and the invention of the first automobile (Oliver Evans).

Watergate Scandal, The

~• It was the Vatican that financed the construction of the Watergate Hotel and Apartment complex in Washington, D.C. which later became the infamous hotel in which the Watergate scandal (1972–74) took place.

~• "Deep Throat" was name of the informant who helped blow open the Watergate scandal. He was so named by the managing editor of the *Washington Post*, Howard Simons, because of the popular pornographic movie of the same name at the time, which itself was causing widespread public controversy.

~• Bob Woodward, the journalist at the Washington Post, said that if he ever wanted to signal "Deep Throat" he would place a flowerpot holding a red flag on the balcony of his apartment.

~• The parking garage that Bob Woodward and Deep Throat would often meet in was located at 1401 Wilson Boulevard, just over the Key Bridge in Rosslyn.

~• Despite taking precautions and meeting in secret, Woodward also admitted that he sometimes just called Deep Throat on the phone at his home.

~• During the final days in the White House of President Richard Nixon (1913–1994), Secretary of State Henry Kissinger made a prediction that history would be kind to Nixon and would remember him as a great president. Kissinger believed that the Watergate incident would eventually become merely a "minor footnote" in American history.

 The break-in at the headquarters of the Democratic National Congress was unusual because the five burglars were carrying $2,300 in 100-dollar bills, lock-picks and door-jimmys, a walkie-talkie, a radio scanner, two cameras, 40 rolls of unused film, tear-gas guns, and certain sophisticated devices capable of recording conversations that might be held in the offices.

 In Woodward's book *All the President's Men*, he said that Deep Throat was an "incurable gossip ... in a unique position to observe the Executive Branch," and someone "whose fight had been worn out in too many battles."

 Richard Nixon is also quoted as saying "When the President does it, that means that it is not illegal."

Whiskey Rebellion

🍂 The Whiskey Rebellion in the 1790s came about as a protest to the tax on whiskey, which had been introduced to help relieve U.S. national debt. That being said, even Alexander Hamilton the treasury secretary who imposed the tax could see that it had its benefits as "a measure of moral discipline."

🍂 The government settled on two ways one could pay the tax, which was either by the gallon or by paying a flat fee. This didn't help the small producers who ended up paying 9 cents a gallon, while the bigger players were only being taxed at 6 cents.

🍂 Because not everyone had the stomach for a rebellion, a little bit of reinforcement was required. Anonymous notes and newspaper articles signed by "Tom the Tinker" were distributed, threatening to burn down the stills of anyone who *did* pay the tax.

🍂 At the time of the Whiskey Rebellion, Kentucky and Tennessee were still outside of federal control and so they kept on distilling with limestone-filtered water and corn, which is how they developed Bourbon.

🍂 The Whiskey Rebellion received a mention much later on in history. In 1962, American singer-songwriter Joan Baez referred to it in the song "Copper Kettle" when she sang, "We ain't paid no whiskey tax since 1792."

William the Conqueror

❧ What's in a name? William the Conqueror (circa 1028–1087) the first Norman King of England was also known as William the Bastard because his parents were unmarried when he was born.

❧ When Duke William of Normandy disembarked from his ship in the lead up to his attack at the Battle of Hastings in 1066, he slipped and fell flat out on the sand. Fearing that his soldiers would take this as an omen he exclaimed, "By the splendor of God, I have taken seisin [possession] of England! I hold its earth in my hands!"

❧ William married Matilda of Flanders. She eventually bore him 11 children, but not before the pope stepped in to express his disapproval of the match because he believed the two were too closely related.

❧ William wasn't the nicest of dads and took pleasure in humiliating his children in public, including calling his first born son *Gambaron* (fat legs).

❧ After 1072, William spent more than 75 percent of his time in France rather than in England. While he needed to be personally present in Normandy to defend the realm from foreign invasion and put down internal revolts, he was able to set up royal administrative structures that enabled him to rule England from a distance by "writ."

🐦 Try as he might, William could never master the language of England (Anglo-Saxon) and, as a result, his native tongue of French remained the language of the court for years to come.

Woodstock

 Prior to the festival weekend, 100,000 tickets were sold, but they were purposeless. The fences and gates were never properly finished and music fans swarmed over the ones that were in place.

 The festival was remarkably safe and only two fatalities were recorded. One death was caused by a heroin overdose and the other death was caused by someone being run over by the tractor they were sleeping under.

 Melanie Safka, an American singer-songwriter didn't have her performer's pass and so had to sing her song "Beautiful People" to the security guards before she was allowed to go backstage.

 Approximately 14 percent of those in the audience at Woodstock were in cohabitating relationships at the time.

 Jimi Hendrix (1942–1970) played a white 1968 Fender Stratocaster at the groundbreaking Woodstock performance that included his scandalous rendition of the "Star-Spangled Banner." The *New York Post* called it, "the single greatest moment of the Sixties," but most of the audience had already left and missed it.

 Joan Baez performed the last song on Friday, August 15, 1969. It was "Swing Low, Sweet Chariot."

 Despite the persisting myth of the "Woodstock Babies", nobody has ever come forward with a birth record showing one existed.

∾ Woodstock was not actually held in Woodstock but on an alfalfa farm in Bethel, New York, as there was nowhere suitable to host the festival in Woodstock itself.

∾ The festival was initially advertised as "A Weekend in the Country."

∾ A Jewish community center heard that there wasn't enough food for the festival goers. The members prepared sandwiches, which were distributed by nuns. In all, 200 loaves of bread, 40 pounds of cold cuts, and two gallons of pickles were used.

World War I

W

⚜ World War I (1914–18) took place in Europe, but most of the world's greatest powers became involved in what developed into one of the deadliest conflicts in history.

⚜ It started with a bang! The murder of the Archduke Franz Ferdinand in Sarajevo is often referred to as the shot heard around the world because it was this event that launched the start of the conflict. In fact, it took several attempts to kill the archduke that day. Seven assassins were sent out to do the hit: the first did nothing; the second threw a bomb at the car but Ferdinand picked it up and threw it out the window (blowing up another car and injuring eight); the third, fourth, fifth, and sixth did nothing. The seventh, Gavrilo Princip, a Bosnian who was part of the Serbian terrorist group plotting to kill the archduke, jumped onto the car Ferdinand was passenger in as he was on his way to visit the injured in a hospital, and shot him.

⚜ Once war was underway, Germans would begin the day by greeting one another with the words "God punish England." They had these words printed on letters, postcards, badges, and brooches.

⚜ The British Security Service, better known as MI5, apparently used Girl Guides to deliver their messages, but made them promise not to read them.

⚜ Poison gas attacks became a common occurrence during in World War I. The advice given to soldiers in instances of a gas attack was to urinate on a piece of cloth, hold it over the face, and breathe through it.

❧ DORA was Britain's Defense of the Realm Act and it stated some rather unusual rules about what NOT to do during the war: no loitering under railroad bridges; no sending letters overseas with invisible ink; no buying binoculars without official permission; no flying of kites that could be used for signaling; no ringing of church bells after sundown; and no whistling in the street for a taxi after 10 P.M., just to name a few.

❧ On Christmas Day 1914, German and British troops called a temporary truce and serenaded each other with Christmas carols from their opposing trenches. A few brave souls even crossed "No-man's Land" to exchange small gifts such as whiskey and cigars.

❧ One of the craziest inventions of World War I was the gun helmet. This was a piece of headgear with a large gun barrel at the front. It was fired by using an air pipe, which was also the chinstrap. Downside? The recoil was so bad it made the soldiers dizzy and disoriented as well as giving them terrible headaches.

❧ Kaiser Wilhelm (1859–1941), monarch of Germany, operated as Commander-in-Chief of the German armed forces throughout the war. He was born with a withered left arm, which he insisted on hiding whenever his photo was taken.

World War II

🐦 Perhaps not having learned what a terrible waste of life war could be after World War I, and hopping mad about the terms of the Treaty of Versailles, the Germans regrouped and decided to try their luck at taking over Europe for the second time. World War II lasted from 1939 to 1945.

🐦 The first bomb dropped by the Allies on Berlin during World War II killed the only elephant in the Berlin Zoo.

🐦 In 1940, in Britain, the Home Guard was the name given to those who were responsible for defense of England's home turf. However, the Home guard were more at risk of being injured or killed by their own weapons than by enemy attack. At the end of the war, 768 had been accidentally killed and nearly 6,000 injured from the misuse and misfiring of weapons.

🐦 Most armies didn't have the right equipment for fighting during winter. The Italians had only cardboard boots as they fought alongside the Germans. So, when they came across dead Russian soldiers with boots frozen to their feet, they would cut the legs off below the knee, carry them back to the camp, and put them in the oven for about 10 minutes. When the limb had defrosted they were able to claim the boots.

🐦 Meanwhile, the Russians and the Japanese both used half-starved dogs as suicide bombers against the enemy. With bombs attached to them, the dogs were trained to look for food under tanks. Once the dog was in the right position, a special pressure trigger detonated the bomb, which tore through the underside of the vehicle.

~● During World War II, the British and Allied troops even had camouflaged toilet paper. (It was khaki brown.)

~● During D-Day (June 6, 1944), when the Allied troops were ferried across the English Channel to storm the beaches at Normandy, condoms were used to cover rifle barrels. This prevented them from being damaged by saltwater as the soldiers swam to shore.

~● During the Battle of the Pacific, a part of World War II that took place in the Pacific Ocean between the Allies and Japan, the number of soldiers that died on the island of Guam provided a feast for the flies. This in turn led the American soldiers to pile on the insect repellent to avoid being bitten. Unfortunately, the repellent smelled so strong that the Japanese were soon able to sniff out U.S. troops in the dark.

~● From 1944 until 1972 Japanese Lieutenant Hiroo Onoda hid in a remote jungle of the Philippines. When he was discovered he refused to surrender because he did not believe that World War II was all over and he could go home.

~● Joseph Goebbels (1897–1945) did become the Führer of Germany, but only for a few hours. Before his death, Hitler had decreed that the German State be left to Goebbels. However, Goebbels was fully aware that he was being surrounded by Soviet forces, so he decided instead to poison his whole family and then kill himself.

Xiaoping, Deng

⌣ Deng Xiaoping (1904–1997) was a Chinese politician, statesman, and diplomat who eventually became leader of the Communist Party of China after the death of Mao Zedong (1893–1976). Reputed to be a talented and intelligent man, he was nicknamed "a living encyclopedia" by those who knew him best.

⌣ Deng is also known as "the architect" of a new kind of socialist thinking having led Chinese economic reform and developing what is called "Socialism with Chinese characteristics."

⌣ Deng was the target of at least seven assassination attempts between 1960 and 1980, most of which remain unsolved.

⌣ After his funeral, Deng's organs were donated to medical research, his remains cremated, and his ashes scattered at sea according to his wishes.

⌣ In 1985, Deng was chosen as *Time* magazine's Man of the Year.

Ypres, Battle of

🔹 There were in fact five Battles of Ypres during World War I. The first was October 19 to November 22, 1914 (also known as the First Battle of Flanders.) The second was April 22 to May 15, 1915. The third was the struggle for Passchendaele, which went on from July 31 to November 6, 1917. The forth was the battle of the Lys, which took place from April 9 to 29, 1918. The fifth and final battle took place from September 28 to October 2, 1918.

🔹 Regiments often had mascots to represent them during World War I and the Scots Guards adopted an unusual pair. Following the battle of Ypres in 1914, only two cows (later named Bella and Bertha) survived the shelling, and they carried on providing the soldiers with fresh milk in the trenches. The beloved bovines were later retired to Scotland, but not before they were marched through London in the Victory Parade after the war had ended.

🔹 While Ypres is pronounced "ee-pruh" most British soldiers called it "Wipers" and in 1915 even came up with a limerick about the place:

> There was a young lady from Ypres (think wipers!)
> who was hit in the cheek by two snipers
> the tune that she played
> through the holes that they made
> beat the Argyll and Sutherland pipers.

Y

 The "Old Contemptibles" were a British Expeditionary Force sent to the front line in World War I. It was Kaiser Wilhelm (1859–1941) who was responsible for their name. He issued an order on August 19, 1914, to "exterminate … the treacherous English and walk over General French's contemptible little army." So the name stuck among the survivors—though they ended up suffering heavy casualties later in the First Battle of Ypres.

 The first gas attacks by the German army caused the launch of the Second Battle of Ypres (April 22, 1915). At around 5 P.M. that day the German Army released 168 tons of chlorine gas over the 4-mile (6.5-km) front. The Germans had to haul 5,730 cylinders to the front. Each weighed 90 lb (40 kg) and had to be opened by hand. The Germans relied on the prevailing winds to blow the gas in the right direction, away from them and at the enemy. Needless to say, thanks to the wind, a number of German soldiers also perished that day.

Yugoslavia

꙳ Yugoslavia was a political and geographic entity that existed in the Balkan region of Europe during the twentieth century. At the end of World War I, the Kingdom of Serbs, Croats, and Slovenes was formed on December 1, 1918 as part of the Versailles Peace Treaties, and was commonly known as a "Versailles State". The idea was to create a great Slav state. They hadn't bargained on the fact that they wouldn't get along.

꙳ The term Yugoslavia was first used under King Alexander I who inherited the throne from his father, King Peter I of Serbia, in 1921. But he ruled absolutely, imposed censorship, and banned flags of the individual nations that made up the country. This made him rather unpopular. He was assassinated while on a visit to France in 1934.

꙳ After World War II, a federal state of six republics was formed: Bosnia-Herzegovina, Croatia, Macedonia, Montenegro, Serbia, and Slovenia. Josip Broz Tito (1892–1980), leader of the Federation of Yugoslavia was perhaps born to do the job because his mother was a Slovene and his father was Croat.

꙳ As a communist leader, Tito was also the only one to ever refuse Stalin and live to tell the tale. He apparently once wrote to Stalin, saying: "Stop sending people to kill me. We've already captured five of them, one of them with a bomb and another with a rifle (…) If you don't stop sending killers, I'll send one to Moscow, and I won't have to send a second." Very brave man...

Y

❧ During Tito's time in power, Yugoslavia had the fifth-strongest army in Europe.

❧ On May 2, 2006, many voters in Montenegro showed up for a referendum to vote on independence from Serbia. According to the EU, a 55 percent majority was required for a "yes" vote to be accepted internationally. The result? 55.5 percent of the Montenegrins voted "yes" and won their independence.

❧ Kosovo is now one of the newest nations of the twenty-first century having declared its independence from Serbia on February 17, 2008, though Serbia still refuses to accept this.

❧ When the White House was built in the U.S., it is said that Croatian stone from the island of Brac was used, the largest island in the Dalmatian group of islands.

Zambia

- The skull of "Rhodesian Man" belonging to the species *Homo heidelbergensis* was found in Kabwe, Zambia in 1921. It is thought to be around 300,000 years old.

- The Scottish missionary and explorer Dr. David Livingstone (1813–1873) named the Victoria Falls after the British queen. In turn, Livingstone was the name given to the capital of Northern Rhodesia, and was used until 1935.

- In 1961, the United Nations Secretary General, Dag Hammarskjold of Sweden, died in a plane crash near Ndola, Zambia.

- After he died of malaria and dysentery in 1873 in Africa, David Livingstone's heart was buried under a Mvula tree at Chitambo. However, his body was buried at Westminster Abbey in London.

- The Copper Belt is not something you use to hold up your pants, but the name given to the area in Zambia near the towns of Ndola, Kitwe, Chingola, Luanshya, which are rich in copper deposits.

Z

Zanzibar

_____ ❦ _____

❧ Even though Zanzibar was incorporated into the United Republic of Tanzania in 1964, it still has its own democratically elected president and government to run the day-to-day affairs of its islands, named Unguj and Pemba.

❧ Knock! Knock! Zanzibar has the largest number of carved doors in East Africa.

❧ In the capital of Stone Town, a building known as the House of Wonders (which was built in 1883 as a ceremonial palace for Sultan Barghash) was the first in Zanzibar to have electric lighting and an electric lift and is still one of the largest buildings in Zanzibar.

❧ Zanzibar took part in the shortest war in history when they fought England in 1896. They surrendered after only 38 minutes of fighting.

❧ Freddie Mercury, the late lead singer of the British band Queen was born in Zanzibar on September 5, 1946.

❧ The capital of Stone Town alone has 50 mosques and four Hindu temples, all for a population of about 700,000.

Z

Zedong, Mao

❧ Mao Zedong (1893–1976) was a military and political leader of the Communist Party of China and the People's Republic of China from 1949 to 1976. Originally he had started out in life training to be a teacher at the Changsha Teacher's School.

❧ The Chinese are big on their astrology and given that Mao was born in the year of the Snake (which is considered a "little dragon") and died in the year of the Dragon, it was considered to be auspicious.

❧ Mao was married four times but his first marriage was not consummated as he was just 14 when he wed. Wife number one was Luo Yixiu (1907–10) who died just a year of marriage. Wife number two was Yang Kai-hui (1920–1930) who was Mao's professor's daughter. Wife number three was He Zizhen (1930–37), a guerilla fighter. Wife number four was Jiang Qing (1939–1976), and she was an actress.

❧ During his Chairmanship, Mao took up residence in a compound next door to the Forbidden City in Beijing. There, he ordered an indoor swimming pool to be built? (he liked swimming) and often took to working either from his bed or the side of the pool, not bothering to get dressed up unless he absolutely had to.

❧ Mao may have liked swimming but he did not like taking a bath, or having a shower, and didn't do so for at least a quarter of a century. Instead he would have servants rub him up and down with hot towels.

Z

◆ Mao had a heart attack on September 2, 1976, and was kept in hospital for some time as his health deteriorated. The last thing he asked for was an update on the Japanese Prime Minister, Takeo Miki, who was facing a coup from within his own party. Mao died at ten minutes past midnight on September 9.

Zhou (Chou) Dynasty

🌿 Lasting 800 years, the Zhou Dynasty (1046–256 B.C.E.) was the most enduring dynasty in Chinese history. In the last 500 years it was in near constant war with itself, a time known as the Warring States Period. In 221 B.C.E. finally it collapsed, which ushered in the Qin Dynasty (221–206 B.C.E.).

🌿 Iron deposits were discovered throughout China during the Zhou Dynasty, enabling the Chinese to produce cast iron a whole millennium before the Europeans.

🌿 The chancellor of Wei, Sunshu Ao, who served King Zhuang of Chu (died 591 B.C.E.), dammed a river to create an enormous irrigation reservoir in what is now modern-day northern Anhui province. As a result Sunshu is credited as China's first hydraulic engineer.

🌿 Hell hath no fury ... in 771 B.C.E. King You, the twelfth emperor of the Zhou Dynasty, deposed his wife, Queen Shen, and their son in favor of his concubine Baosi. However, Queen Shen's father, the Marquess of Shen, was a very powerful man. As revenge he had the capital sacked, the king and his son by Baosi killed, and his grandson, Ji Yijiu, proclaimed the new king.

🌿 The religion followed by those living in the time of the Zhou Dynasty taught that there was one god, and that he held the entire world in his hand.

Z

❧ Human sacrifices were a common occurrence in the Zhou dynasty. The Marquis Yi of Zeng was found to have had 21 women buried with him in his tomb, eight of whom were found in his burial chamber. It also contained the largest cache of ancient musical instruments ever found.

❧ During the Zhou Dynasty, military victories were celebrated by presenting the captors to the emperor and then sacrificing them in an ancestral temple. The next day, the meat from the sacrifices was cooked and eaten.

❧ The famous book on warfare by Chinese military general Sun Tzu, *The Art of War* (6th century B.C.E.), was written during the Zhou Dynasty. The Chinese had been fighting one another constantly for some 500 years so there was a wealth of local knowledge for him to draw on! Since then it has become an international bestseller. It is considered essential reading for many business schools, and has even been made into a Hollywood movie starring Wesley Snipes, though it is only loosely based on the book.

Zimbabwe

◦❧ Zimbabwe was formerly known as Southern Rhodesia, named after English businessman Cecil Rhodes (1853–1902). Rhodes worked for the British South Africa Company and, following a war with local tribes over access to mineral deposits, took over the land.

◦❧ The name Zimbabwe has been derived from *Dzimba dza mabwe* in the Shona language, which means "great houses of stone."

◦❧ "Blessed be the Land of Zimbabwe" is the national anthem of Zimbabwe.

◦❧ The two main traditional symbols of Zimbabwe are the Zimbabwe Bird and the Balancing Rocks. Others include the flame lily and the Sable Antelope.

◦❧ The Khami ruins, one of Zimbabwe's UNESCO World Heritage Sites, is said to contain ancient artifacts from as far away as Europe and China.

◦❧ The Victoria Falls in Zimbabwe are locally known as *Mosi-oa-Tunya*, "the smoke that thunders."

◦❧ Even though they were officially boycotting the 1980 Olympic Games in Moscow, Zimbabwe still won the gold medal in field hockey.

Z

❧ The small group of Vadoma people of western Zimbabwe are more commonly known as the "ostrich people" or "the two-toes tribe." Because of a genetic condition, known as ectrodactyly, the middle three toes of their feet are missing.

❧ Back in 1964, Robert Mugabe, born in 1924 and current President of Zimbabwe, was arrested for subversive speech. He spent the next 11 years in prison in Harare where he gained three degrees, one of which was a law degree from the University of London.

❧ Mugabe has received more than 50 honorary degrees from various institutions. However, the University of Edinburgh and the University of Massachusetts have both taken away the honorary degrees they awarded him due to his recent record of human right violations.

Zoroastrianism

 For some 1,000 years, Zoroastrianism was one of the most powerful religions in the world in Persia (just before the 6th century B.C.E.), but is now one of the world's smallest religions. In 2006, the *New York Times* reported that there were probably fewer than 190,000 followers worldwide at that time.

 Founded by the Prophet Zoroaster (eighteenth to the tenth century B.C.E.), who is also known as Zarathustra, his ideas and beliefs were slow to catch on and at first he only had one convert—his cousin Maidhyoimanha.

 Today's Zoroastrians (aka Parsis) practice an important coming of age ritual. All young Parsis, upon reaching the age of seven (in India) or 10 (in Persia) must be initiated. They receive the *sadre* (shirt) and the *kusti* (girdle), which they are to wear their whole life.

 During the service, married female relatives hold a fine scarf (nowadays usually white) over the couple's heads. At the same time two crystallized sugar cones are rubbed together, to sweeten the couple's life.

 Zoroastrians do not convert other people, but rely on marriage within and increased birth rates to increase their numbers.

 He wants to break free ... Few people realize that the legendary rock star Freddie Mercury was born into a devout Zoroastrian family, but he was not actively religious as an adult.

Z

When Zoastrians die, their remains are taken to a Tower of Silence. The interior of the tower is based on three concentric circles. There is one each for men, women, and children. The corpses are left there, naked and exposed so that vultures can swoop down to strip the flesh off the bones. Once the bones have been dried by the sun, they are swept into the central well of the building.

Bibliography

Anzovin, Steven & Podell, Janet. *Famous First Facts: International Edition: A Record of First Happenings, Discoveries, and Inventions in World History*, H. W. Wilson, 2000.

Axelrod, Alan. *The International Encyclopedia of Secret Societies and Fraternal Orders (Facts on File)*, New York: Checkmark Books, 1997.

Bergreen, Laurence. *Marco Polo: From Venice to Xanadu*, London, UK: Quercus, 2007.

Blashfield, Jean F. *Ireland: Enchantment of the World*, Children's Press, Scholastic, New York: 2002.

Borthwick, Mark. *Pacific Century: The Emergence of Modern Pacific Asia*, Boulder, CO: Westview Press, 2006.

Botkins, Daniel B. *No Man's Garden: Thoreau and a New Vision for Civilization and Nature*, Washington: Island Press. 2001.

Bowen, HV. *War and British Society 1688–1815*, Cambridge, UK: Cambridge University Press, 1998.

Bushnell, David and Langley, Lester D. *Simón Bolívar: Essays on the Life and Legacy of the Liberator*, Lanham, Rowman, & Littlefield, 2008.

Carpenter, David. *The Struggle for Mastery: The Penguin History of Britain 1066–1284*, New York: Penguin, 2004.

Caselli, Giovanni. *In Search of Tutankhamun*, Peter Bedrick Books, 1999.

Chang, Jung, Jon Halliday. *Mao: The Unknown Story*, London, UK: Jonathan Cape, 2007.

Chodorow, Stanley, Macgregor Knox, Conrad Schirokauer, Joseph R. Strayer, Hans W. Gatzke, eds. *The Mainstream of Civilization*, 6th ed. Fort Worth, TX: The Harecourt Press, 1994.

Cohen, Alexei J. Venice, *Moon Handbooks*, Berkeley, CA: Perseus Books Group, 2008.

Crisp, Peter. *Ancient Rome: History in Art*, Oxford, UK: Raintree Publishers, 2006.

Croddy, Eric. *Chemical and Biological Warfare: A Comprehensive Guide for the Concerned Citizen,* 1st ed. London, UK: Springer, 2001.

Crofton, Ian. *History without the Boring Bits,* London, UK: Quercus Publishing, 2007.

Cross, Robin. *The Battle of the Bulge 1944: Hitler's Last Hope,* Gloucestershire, UK: The History Press, 2002.

Crystal, David. *The Stories of English,* New York: The Overlook Press, 2004.

Davies, John, Nigel Jenkins. *The Welsh Academy Encyclopaedia of Wales,* Cardiff, Wales: University of Wales Press, 2008.

Deary, Terry. *Horrible Histories Series,* London, UK: Scholastic.

Deem, James M. *Bodies from the Ash,* Boston: Houghton Mifflin Company, 2005.

Dodge, Christine Huda. *The Everything Understanding Islam Book,* Cincinnati: Adams Media, 2009.

Elkin, Judith Laikin. *The Jews of Latin America,* The University of North Carolina Press, 1980.

Feinberg, Barbara Silberdick. *America's First Ladies: Changing Expectations,* New York: Franklin Watts, 1998.

Feinstein, Stephen. *The 1930s: From the Great Depression to the Wizard of Oz,* Revised Ed. Berkeley Heights, NJ: Enslow Publishers, Inc., 2006.

Fox, Deborah. *How Do We Know about the Gunpowder Plot?* Oxford, UK: Heinemann Library, 2007.

Gascoigne, Bamber. *The Dynasties of China: A History,* New York: Carroll & Graf Publishers, 2003.

Gates, Henry Louis; Anthony Appiah. *Africana: The Encyclopedia of the African and African American Experience,* New York: Basic Civitas Books, 1999.

Geldart, Anne. *Christianity,* Oxford, UK: Heinemann Library, 2000.

Gifford, Clive. *10 Kings and Queens who Changed the World,* London, UK: Kingfisher Books, 2009.

Gleason, Abbott. *A Companion to Russian History,* Chichester, UK: Wiley, 2009.

Hakim, Joy. *The Story of Science, Aristotle Leads the Way,* Washington: Smithsonian Books, 2004.

Halberstam, David. *The Coldest Winter: America and the Korean War,* New York: Disney Hyperion, 2007.

Harrison, James. *The Kingfisher Children's Encyclopedia of British History,* London, UK: Kingfisher Books, 2005.

Haugen, Paul. *World History for Dummies,* IDG Books, 2001.

Hoefnagel, Marian. *Anne Frank: Her Life,* London, UK: Evans Brothers, 2009.

Hogeland, William. *The Whiskey Rebellion: George Washington, Alexander Hamilton, and the Frontier Rebels Who Challenged America's New found Sovereignty,* New York: Scribner, 2006.

Holden, Lynn. *Encyclopedia of Taboos,* Denver, Colorado: ABC-CLIIO, 2000.

Hutchinson Encyclopedia, 11th ed. Oxford, UK: Helicon Publishing Ltd.

January, Brendan. *Amazing Explorers,* The New York Public Library, New York: John Wiley & Sons, Inc., 2001.

Kane, Joseph Nathan. *Famous First Facts,* 6th Edition., New York: The Howard Wilson Company, 2006.

Knecht, R. J. *Catherine de' Medici,* London and New York: Longman, 1998.

Kurian, Thomas ed. *The Illustrated Book of World Rankings,* 5th ed., Sharpe Reference, 2001.

Langley, Andrew. *The Oxford Children's Book of Famous People,* 3rd ed. Oxford, UK: Oxford University Press, 2002.

Lee, A.D. "The Empire at War". *The Cambridge Companion to the Age of Justinian,* Michael Maas (ed.). Cambridge, UK: Cambridge University Press, 2005

Lenman, Bruce P, consultant. *Chambers Dictionary of World History,* 2nd ed. London, UK: Chambers, 2000.

Levy, Pat. *From Speakeasies to Stalinism,* Chicago: Raintree, 2005.

Levy, Pat. *From Television to the Berlin Wall,* Chicago: Raintree, 2005.

Ling, Peter J. *Martin Luther King, Jr.* Abingdon, Oxford, UK: Routledge, 2002.

Lowe, Norman. *Mastering Modern World History,* 4th ed., London, UK: Palgrave Macmillan, 2005.

Macdonald, Fiona. *You Wouldn't Want to be Married to Henry VIII,* London, UK: Hodder Wayland, 2002.

Malam, John. *5 November 1605: The Gunpowder Plot,* London, UK: Cherrytree Books, 2003.

Marchant, Kerena. *Great Religious Leaders: Krishna and Hinduism,* London, UK: Wayland, 2002.

Matthews, Rupert. *Ancient Greece,* Great Bardfiled, Essex, UK: Miles Kelly Publishing, 2007.

McWhorter, Diane. *Carry Me Home: Birmingham, Alabama, The Climactic Battle of the Civil Rights Revolution,* New York: Touchstone Book, 2002.

Medvedev, Zhores, A. Roy A. Medvedev. *The Unknown Stalin,* London, UK: I.B. Tauris, 2003.

Mentzel, Peter. *A Traveller's History of Venice,* Intelink Books, NH, 2006.

Michael, Axworthy. *The Sword of Persia: Nader Shah, from Tribal Warrior to Conquering Tyrant,* London, UK: I.B. Tauris, 2006.

Montefiore, Simon Sebag. *101 Heroes of an Unheroic Age*, London, UK: Quercus, 2008.

Nash, Gary B. *The Unknown American Revolution: The Unruly Birth of Democracy and the Struggle to Create America*, New York: Viking, 2005.

Overy, Richard. *The Battle of Britain*, London, UK: Penguin Books, 2010.

Parker, Steven and Williams, Brian. *Question and Answer Encyclopedia: World History*, Essex, UK: Miles Kelly Publishing, 2004.

Penney, Sue. *Introducing Religions Series*. Oxford, UK: Heinemann Library, 2007.

Peron, James E. *Woodstock: An Encyclopedia of the Music and Art Festival*, Westport, CT: Greenwood Press, 2005.

Picard, Liza. *Elizabeth's England*, New York: St. Martin's Press, 2003.

Platt, Richard. *Pompeii*, Kingfisher, 2007.

Poole, Josephine and Barrett, Angela. *Anne Frank*, London, UK: Red Fox, 2007.

Quarles, Chester L. *The Ku Klux Klan and Related Racialist and Antisemitic Organizations: An Overview*, Jefferson, NC: McFarland, 1999.

Quinn, Tom. *Military's Strangest Campaigns and Characters*, London, UK: Portico, 2006.

Roberts, J. M. *The Penguin History of Europe*, London, UK: Penguin. 2004.

Ross, Stewart. *Oxford Children's Book of the 20th Century*, Oxford, UK: Oxford University Press, 1998.

Sabin, Philip A G; Van Wees, Hans; and Whitby, Michael. *The Cambridge History of Greek and Roman Warfare*, Cambridge, UK: Cambridge University Press, 2007.

Sorensen, Ted. *Counselor: A Life at the Edge of History*, New York: HarperCollins Publishers, 2008.

Spence, Jonathan D. (1999). *The Search for Modern China*, 2nd ed. New York: W.W. Norton & Company, 1999.

Spignesi, Stephen S. *The 100 Greatest Disasters of All Time*, New York: Citadel Press, 2002.

Stephens, John Richards. *Weird History 101*, Adams Media, 1997.

Stokesbury, James L. *A Short History of the Korean War*, New York: Harper Perennial, 1990.

Sugden, John. *Nelson: A Dream of Glory*, London, UK: Jonathan Cape, 2004.

Tames, Richard. *Adolf Hitler*, Oxford, UK: Heinemann Library, 1999.

Thomas J. Johnson. *Watergate and the Resignation of Richard Nixon: Impact of a Constitutional Crisis*, Thomas Maxwell-Long and P. Jeffrey, eds. Washington, D.C.: CQ Press, 2004.

Wright, David Curtis. *The History of China*, Santa Barbara, CA: Greenwood Publishing Group, 2001.